AF574686

FROM BRADMAN TO BOYCOTT

THE MASTER BATSMEN

By the same author

Ted Dexter's Cricket Book
Ted Dexter Declares
Testkill
The Deadly Putter

FROM BRADMAN TO BOYCOTT

THE MASTER BATSMEN

TED DEXTER

Queen Anne Press
Macdonald Futura Publishers
London

First published in 1981 by Queen Anne Press,
Macdonald Futura Publishers Limited, Paulton House,
8 Shepherdess Walk, London N1 7LW

ISBN 0354 08560 3

Printed and bound in Great Britain
by Mackays of Chatham Ltd

CONTENTS

INTRODUCTION

Curvaceous, pale-skinned and perfectly proportioned, a cricket bat of good pedigree can arouse the instinct of a connoisseur as surely as any other work of art. In the mass, of course, like human beings, these wooden cudgels are all much of a muchness; not a lot to pick between them. But lay eyes on the genuine article, gauge the grain, run your hand over the rise and fall of its contoured back and experience the mystery of perfect balance. It takes little genius then to know that this is no mundane thing.

I know I am not alone in my recollections of the first bat to belong to me. I cleaned and oiled that Len Hutton autograph size 3, treble spring, with all the loving care of a young girl tending her first pony. It may have been a Gunn and Moore or perhaps a Gradidge but it is the colour and feel of that pampered bat that I remember most and, young as I was, it was not long before I discovered that with bats, at any rate, it is the best looker which is most likely to have a heart of gold.

The Laws of Cricket are wonderfully brief in laying down what kind of implement should be used for the game. 'The bat shall not exceed 4¼in/10.8cm, in the widest part. It shall not be more than 38in/96.5cm in length.' That is all. There is no restriction on the depth, nor on the weight, and only recently on the material from which it may be made. So it is a tribute to the early bat makers that, despite much research by manufacturers into possible alternatives, their original products have barely been improved upon in over one hundred years. The present width was fixed as long ago as 1771, the length in 1835. Cane handles were invented by a Mr Nixon in 1853 approximately, and rubber handle-covers were patented in 1880. All these basic elements survive today, the most basic of all being the wood itself.

Willow, English willow, is the substance universally adopted for its unique properties: absorbing shock, enduring literally thousands of blows from the hard cork, twine, and leather ball, and, at the same time, propelling the ball at great speed (when wielded by the right hands). Nobody has so far come up with any kind of acceptable substitute and, even if they did, there would be such strong sales resistance that I would doubt its commercial chances. Perhaps the strongest argument against innovation would centre on the importance of the right sound, the traditional noise of bat on ball. I can imagine the spluttering consternation in the front row of the Members' seats at Lord's if the afternoon tranquillity were disturbed by some foreign clicking from the middle instead of the anticipated lulling thump.

New ideas have been limited to alternative weight distribution at the back of the bat; a scoop down the middle can allow more wood at the edges and a variation of that theme has been tried, using the engineering principle of 'drilling-out'. Binding with vellum is also done to prolong active life but this incurs an unacceptable weight penalty, quite apart from the less attractive look of the thing. Denis Lillee attempted to use a bat of aluminium in a Test match but fell foul of the umpires immediately.

Unquestionably the greatest preoccupation of the modern batsman is, or should be, the overall balance, where the variable factors are the thickness of the handle, its length, the all-up weight, and the way that weight is distributed. Science has done little to assist cricketers in this crucial matter of choice, whereas golfers can resort to all sorts of available data on swing-weight and shaft dynamics. And this may be the moment to point to the enormous amount of legislation forced upon the Royal and Ancient Golf Club to safeguard traditional golf club making against the wilder fringe of inventions which continually threaten to turn golf into something nearer rifle shooting. The cricket authorities can count themselves fortunate to be spared this particular nuisance, and can bless the enduring properties of willow for their deliverance.

Reverting to the wood itself, the points to look for are simple enough. Somewhere between milk and cream is about the right colour, five to nine lines of grain are quite acceptable, and there should be no prejudice against 'butterflies' – delicate, lace-like marking which should not be confused with the round or oblong fault, typical of actual knots. Finally there is the smell of the bat, but that must inevitably be a matter of personal preference, especially when I tell you that the final lustre was for years imparted by rubbing the willow to a sheen with the shin-bone of a horse.

As in life itself, there is no substitute for experience and even then it is not impossible to make a fool of oneself. There is always going to be the bat which has all the hallmarks of quality and yet turns out to be a damp squib. At the moment of realisation there is nothing for it but to offload the brute on to some innocent tail-ender and trust that he never notices. Similarly, if you happen to pick up a bat which bounces a ball on the face as though it were made of rubber, then that is the bat to hang on to whether or not it looks right, always assuming that it picks up easily and lightly. This is the quality which perpetually defies analysis and can really only be investigated by trial and error. The expert obviously has the advantage if his supplier produces a selection to choose from, but even the high street shopper can expect to be confronted with a reasonable range, and the golden rule is simply to pick the one that feels right.

Fashions come and go in the matter of weight, which can vary by as much as one pound in a total of three, but the majority of the great players have tended to use lighter bats than their less successful contemporaries. The exception to that rule, which certainly provides convincing proof that all things are possible, was the prolific Sobers who could wave a three-pound bat round his head like a wand and still have time to spare when the ball came along. I make the point about time because the acknowledged hall-mark of class amongst batsmen is the impression which they convey that there is all the time in the world to decide what they want to do with the ball before they actually do it. As it is possible to move a light object more quickly than a heavier one over a given distance, it is logical to link the time-weight equation with the preference of the best players for bats of two pounds three ounces to two pounds seven ounces; any lighter, and the ball starts to feel too heavy to hit, but further up the weight scale it simply becomes a matter of strength to wield the bat.

So much for the new bat and how it should look and feel, but there is no doubt that the cricket bat enjoys its finest hour after a certain amount of use; when the blade starts to 'bow' or 'scoop' about five inches from the end; when a few razor-blade scrapings and smears of linseed oil have combined to produce the equivalent of the well run-in motor car. There can be few more specific feelings of harmony than that between a master batsman and this surprising amalgam of willow, Sarawak cane, rubber, and glue, and it would be an achievement as well as a pleasure if something of that feeling flows to readers by the time the rest of this batting story is told.

From the basic principles of the bat itself, it is no great leap to the basic principles of batting, but, before embarking on that hefty subject, I feel that there is much to be gained from studying exactly what the role of the batsman is, and specifically the extent to which this differs from most other games where an implement is used to hit a ball. It is certainly no use making any sweeping generalisation such as 'the role of the batsman is to make runs' when one of the most faithfully recorded statistics refers to how long a batsman manages to stay at the crease without scoring at all. No more can you say that his prime objective is not to be bowled out when many a batsman has been praised for sacrificing his wicket in the chase for runs.

In tennis it is a matter of playing the ball over the net into a prescribed area. In golf, there is the abiding necessity to urge the ball into the hole in as few strokes as possible. The list of simplistic formulae for similar games is a long one but I have yet to find anything both short and comprehensive about batting. The variety of possibilities is so wide for the man with the bat in his hand once the bowler releases the ball in his direction, that it would be a bold man who tried to list them, let alone to claim that he knew them all.

Obviously the first requirement is to survive each individual delivery and be ready to continue the battle when the next one comes along. This can be achieved most effectively by leaving the ball completely alone, and that seemingly simple procedure can only be achieved regularly and successfully if the batsman concerned is entirely certain that the ball will not hit the wicket. To have that certainty when the ball is swerving its way down the pitch at anything up to one hundred miles per hour, is, in itself, a considerable feat of judgement and gives rise to one of the most sought after compliments, i.e. that so-and-so 'really knows where his stumps are'. In practice, however, there are many ways of leaving the ball alone, including lifting the bat out of harm's way, letting the ball hit you on the body, allowing it to pass behind your legs, ducking out from under, or, more correctly, swaying the head and body away from the line. Any one of these actions, and, occasionally, employing more than one at a time, can be correct in given circumstances.

All of this only applies if the ball is palpably off target, but it must be assumed in good class cricket that the majority of bowling will be accurate enough to need at least some pretence of activity from the bat. At this stage the permutations of alternatives becomes considerably wider. Where you hit the ball, and how hard you hit it, is absolutely at your discretion, and, as long as no catcher intervenes between the impact of ball on bat and it falling to earth, the first objective is reached. That there is a grey area between actually playing the ball with the bat and allowing it to hit the body while going through the motions with the bat will be developed as a subject on its own, when the complexities of the leg-before-wicket law are delved into in due course. Meanwhile, it may be enough to consider the strange fact that any two batsmen will almost certainly apply a totally different stroke to the same ball, and will then be prefectly willing to argue that their own decision was the right one in the circumstances. It is hard to think of another ball game where this could so often be the case, and, it is not until one thinks of the more intellectual games, such as chess or bridge, that the same wide area of choice exists.

This opportunity for individuality gives cricket much, if not most, of its charm, and can surely account for the extraordinary cross-section of people from all walks of life to whom the game appeals. In every batsman there is likely to be some particular trait with which the spectator can identify, whether it means admiring grit and persistence, or revelling in the sheer audacity of a great hitter once he gets the bit between his teeth. More different characters than Bradman, Compton or Pataudi (the younger) would be hard to find in a novel, let alone in real life, and yet they all found the art and practice of batting a perfect medium for expressing their personalities. *Vive la différence*, say I, because without it there would be little to write about and even less to savour.

It is, of course, this same sense of variety which has tempted me to select a number of batting categories, and thus to pin a label of a sort on each of the great players who form the subject matter of this book. I am aware of the pitfalls in this approach and the chance it will give critics to doubt my sanity, but some basis of comparison seemed to me to be essential, and without this device I could think of no starting point. Perish the thought, for instance, that these men of such varied gifts should appear in order of the number of runs scored, when that statistic usually indicates nothing more than the length of career. Number of innings and averages also have their weak points because it is just as likely that a player will have missed a season of good, or bad, pitches through illness or injury, just as there is no measurement of the strength of the opposition built into any such mathematical formula.

Neither is it really practical to list these great batsmen in exact chronological order, because the impact of one career is made early in one life and later in another, so actual ages or dates of first appearances are of no great importance. Nevertheless, a rough historical sequence will be maintained without any further attempt to impose a pecking order. With luck the skill and style of each individual will speak for itself, and it is for each reader to decide on his or her own favourites.

To go back to the business of batting itself, there are just a few, a very few, known quantities which the batsman can be sure of before he embarks on the massive task of sifting the list of variables. The dimensions of the pitch–just twenty-two yards long–the height and size of the stumps, and the pitch markings he can take for granted; also the size and weight of the ball, but that is the extent of the basic information with which he has to work before tangling with the unknown.

Take the plight of an opening batsman, whose captain has won the toss in an away match and decided to take first innings. It is entirely possible that our gallant player has never laid eyes on his opening partner, on whom ultimately so much may depend. The ground may be entirely foreign, the pitch, as always, an unknown quantity, and the eleven strangers ranged against him in the field could just as well be thirteen, given that the umpires are local men, too.

There has of course been no practice other than a perfunctory knock-up on the outfield. Our hero taps the pitch inquisitively to gain an inkling of its bounce characteristic, sniffs the air for humidity and wind direction, surveys the deployment of fielders, and makes ready to defend his wicket against all comers. It is hardly the preparation recommended for a combatant who, if his heart's desire were known, is hoping to remain undefeated for the remainder of the day.

Before he receives the first ball, the umpire has been gracious enough to assist him in the elementary matter of 'taking guard', and will also pass on priceless information relating to which arm is to be used for propulsion, and which side of the wicket the assailant will come from. All else remains a secret until the first ball comes out of the bowler's hand, slices deceptively through the air currents, and then leaps or skids off the turf towards the man with the bat in his hand.

It is the moment of truth, the moment of decision. To do nothing is to invite ridicule from the assembled company if it results in being clean bowled or provides the umpire with an obvious case of leg before wicket. On the other hand to do something positive means a deliberate choice, with full knowledge that the result can be equally fatal. Here is the basic dilemma of batting. The fear of getting out grips you long before you ever reach the crease. It sits at your elbow all your cricketing life and regulates your every action. It accounts entirely for the generations of hefty strikers in the nets who are reduced to making impotent pushes and prods in the middle.

Fear of getting out is the gremlin, the ghost with which every batsman must live, and they are a chosen few who can respectfully look that fear in the eye and dismiss it from their mind and muscle. How much this depends on confidence born of success and how much on sheer bravado varies from man to man, but the ability to set aside the possible consequences and to be optimistic about the outcome of positive action is certainly a necessary trait in those who hope to bat long and well.

Happily the first ball in batting is almost invariably the worst. Every succeeding delivery that can be survived constitutes an additional element in programming the human computer. From rank uncertainty, through relative stability to total dominance, an innings can demonstrate much of human life's varied pattern in the space of only an hour or two, which may well account for the game's fascination for so many people. Getting out is a kind of death. Getting runs is better than being a millionaire.

Fascinating is only one of many words to describe the process of batting as it unfolds to the player himself. At first there is the considered application of defensive technique, the loosely held dead bat simply stopping the ball in its path. Any ball wide of the wicket may be left alone and studied closely for behaviour patterns on its way past. The batting process at this stage is watchful, drastically curtailed, and full of apprehension.

Soon must come the difficult transition. For a little while, even the easiest ball must be treated with care while eye and muscle attune themselves, for there is only one thing worse than getting out early to a good ball, and that is getting out early to a bad one. But the need for runs soon presses and now decisions have to be made. Is there a quick single to mid-wicket? And even if there is, will your partner respond if you call him? Should an attempt be made to score off the present steady bowling, or will there be some easy stuff to come later?

The problems for the batsman are legion if only because he has so many alternatives. For instance, I can think of no other game involving implement and ball at which it is possible to score throughout the full three hundred and sixty degrees. There is every angle available from the straight hit to the most delicate deflection, and the greatest players are sometimes capable of playing one or the other at will, with all the possible variations in between, to any and every ball. They certainly set a standard to which it is hard for ordinary mortals to aspire.

Then there is the lurking danger and mystery of the leg-before-wicket law to be dealt with. Leg-before-wicket is an unsatisfactory form of dismissal because it is never a matter of fact, only opinion. Who is to say that the straightest ball might not suddenly swerve at the last second – or even pass through the stumps. Nevertheless it is a necessary evil, to stop batsmen simply kicking the ball away with pads like pumpkins. Since the advent of pads strong enough to shield shins and knees from the ball, the temptation to the defensively-minded player to use these broader obstructions as a first line of defence has been overwhelming.

In 'modern' cricket, up to 1937, the ball was required to 'pitch' in the line of the stumps (and to be hitting) to gain an lbw decision. The effect was to encourage bowlers to deliver from close to the stumps, to swing and spin the ball from leg to off. The batsman stood beside the stumps, the ball came down his off-side and the opportunity for stroke-play was evident – he had room to hit the ball.

Unfortunately, a few defensive players ruined this nice equation, by padding away anything that pitched fractionally wide on the off. The law was changed to admit lbw to such a ball providing the point of contact was still in line – and then it was changed again in 1980 to admit contact outside the off stump where there is 'no attempt to play the ball' with the bat.

The intention has been to direct bowling more to the off-side. That it has done. But damage has arisen to the whole principle of a simple bat and ball game, in that the angle – or line of the ball – is now generally slanted into the body rather than alongside it or away from it. It follows that there is less room to hit the ball and less freedom in stroke-play.

It has caused an imbalance between right and left-handed batsmen, at least for as long as the majority of bowlers are right-handed. In a recent Test match, England v West Indies at Leeds 1980, four right-handed England batsmen fell lbw to fast, short-of-a-length balls from a right-hand bowler, over the wicket. In each case the ball stayed low enough and cut back enough from outside the off-stump to give the umpire grounds for his decision. Had these batsmen been left-handed, the decision would have been reversed on the grounds that the ball pitched outside the leg stump. The law remains illogical.

Batsmen are unwise to hook unless they are sure the ball will bounce above stump height – they are forced to play more off the front foot; hence less stroke-play and the introduction of the helmet as the head is thrust unduly early into the danger zone. The present lbw law has much to answer for in brutalising and diminishing the variety of the game, and in reducing stroke-play and coarsening the batting art.

The original law before 1937 was correct in principle. The addition of the 1980 element only at that time, plus a widening of the stumps perhaps, would have maintained equilibrium better between bat and ball. The very best batsmen seem to have overcome the problems to a remarkable degree, but I doubt that batting is as much fun for the majority as once it was.

Darwin's theory of the survival of the fittest is amply demonstrated in the business of batting, and I hope that this will be shown as I pass comment on so many great players in the following text. I have discussed technique and peculiarities at some length in relation to specific players, their strengths and weaknesses, so I will not pre-empt all that by going into such detail now. However, what does seem appropriate here is to include the text of a talk I was asked to give to the Test and County Cricket Board's seminar for first-class county and National Cricket Association coaches in early 1980. For that daunting occasion I found myself forced to distil all my thoughts on the basic techniques of (right-handed) batsmanship. The extent to which the great batsmen, past, present, and future, adhere to my first principles is for you to judge.

INTRODUCTION

Gentlemen, I would rather take guard against Holding and Roberts than face such a well-informed gathering of cricketers. Against them I could be reasonably certain of a quick dismissal from the middle – whereas here I am sentenced to a full fifteen minutes, however badly I perform. It is a daunting task but at least your combined authority ensures against my preaching a sermon. In essence I want this talk on batting to come over as less of a Commercial, more of a starting point towards a Union of minds. (*The TCCB seminar was sponsored by the Commercial Union Assurance Company Ltd.*)

Our brief today is to try to reach broad agreement on standards – tomorrow to consider ways of implementing them – and I make no apology for going back to basic principles first, because, if we cannot agree on those, the rest is that much harder. It is the variety of methods being tried which I find alarming; as though there is a frantic search for some new panacea, long before it has been proved that the old standards are outdated. The nub of my case today is that we should re-examine traditional methods and cling to them unless convinced they are wrong.

There are clearly alternatives in the search for excellence in batting because no two good players are ever entirely alike. However, I don't remember a good player who did everything contrary to the book. There are common denominators in success, just as I have lately detected common denominators in those who fail to reach their apparent potential. It is my belief that a considerable number of batsmen have the talent – the ball-sense, call it what you will – to be top-class. That so very few make it may well reflect more on their coaches than on themselves.

The most important physical elements in batting seem to me to be: the head and eyes; the upper body; the legs and feet; the hands and bat.

The head and eyes

So here goes. Starting with the head and eyes, it is logical that the head should start on the line where the ball is most likely to come, i.e. around off-stump. However, the latest extension of the lbw law has led to more fast bowling from wide, pitching wide. There is a requirement to play the ball wider – therefore it may well be correct to take guard further to the off than before against this type of bowling. Some flexibility in position should be considered.

Once the stance is taken then the head must obviously turn to get the best possible sight of the ball. It is perhaps equally logical that this head position should be relaxed and comfortable. To achieve this I believe that the shoulders must be slightly open in the stance. I do not believe that perfectly level eyes are strictly necessary, although a badly dropped head would clearly come into the cardinal sin category. Of course the head should remain steady even during the stroke or any other body movement. If there is another cardinal sin in relation to the head and eyes, it is unnecessary movement before and during the stroke.

The upper body

From a slightly open shoulder position, therefore, in the stance, the proper pick-up can bring the body into the desired sideways position for play. Mechanically, it is only possible to play the ball underneath the body, as opposed to out in front of it, by adopting this sideways position. Furthermore only in the sideways position can the defensive stroke develop naturally into the attacking one without alteration. The cardinal sin for the upper body is surely when it starts rigorously sideways only to finish disappointingly square-on.

The legs and feet

Good initial balance is obviously essential but thereafter there are only two possibilities, i.e. either forward or back, although this movement must be across to the line of the ball in each case.

The front foot seems largely to take care of itself, although the nearer to the line of the ball the better; and – another point – too large a stride can be counter-productive by reducing height, reducing bat leverage and pulling the head down. It is the back foot position that matters so much. I have hardly seen a fine player whose back foot does not stay roughly parallel to the batting crease – and I implore you, gentlemen, to make this a lynchpin of your instruction at all levels.

The importance of good footwork hardly needs stressing but what makes the whole system work well is measured movement, up and down and across a narrow rectangle (or bath), as opposed to a tendency to have both feet wedged firmly into a small circle (or chamber pot).

There is one apparent myth which I would like to query which is the on-drive played off the front foot with the left leg splayed out. Close observation of the best players indicate that, whereas on the off-side the feet must move to the line of the ball whether playing forward or back, the more the line of the ball is angled towards the body, the more the ball must be allowed to come on, *without the front leg getting in the way*. The only way to achieve this is to *wait* long enough to see what is happening! It follows, therefore, that the cardinal sin for legs and feet is to move them too early. There is also the sin of going over too far – to be bowled behind the legs or to be caught down the leg-side. Showing the inside edge outside the line of the pads is clearly another cardinal error.

The hands and bat

I see no advantage in using other than the classical grip – although good players have clearly used so-called stronger grips. In any case, to achieve all round stroke-play, i.e. in the horizontal as well as in the vertical plane, it is obvious that an open blade in the pick-up is necessary for mechanical efficiency. Furthermore I put it to you that it is far better for the pick-up to go to second slip than to leg slip, if we are looking at alternatives.

Then, to achieve good timing, the bat end must also be raised above the hands – a fact which probably explains the old adage about 'hitting your way out of a lean patch'. It may be the fact that thinking 'hit' produces more back-lift and thus more strokes and better timing. I believe, further, that only from this open and out position with a good back-lift is it possible to swing the bat truly, as opposed to pushing it. But this, of course, largely depends on maintaining the appropriate body position.

So much for the basic technique – with the overall picture showing us a man standing relaxed, with a steady head, the upper body slightly open until it moves more sideways into the stroke. Each ball will involve a movement forward and back, across to the ball-line on the off-side, letting it come up on the line of the legs. He will be lifting and opening the bat with a view to swinging it when possible and moving late, into the bargain. Neither an early pick-up nor an early foot movement has anything to recommend it. They can both be considered cardinal sins.

Gentlemen, I believe most good players have been taught these essentials – and even if Gary Sobers or Sir Donald Bradman were virtually self-taught, that fact has not stopped them from trying to relay the importance of good technique to succeeding generations.

Fast bowling

It is a natural step now to consider playing different types of bowling, from fast to medium to slow. If I gloss over medium and slow somewhat hurriedly, it is because I believe they largely require the basic virtues of picking length first and adopting good footwork next.

Very fast bowling is another game altogether. Survival, without taking too many damaging blows, is the first essential, and, of course, a preponderance of back play is inevitable, especially these days. I make a special plea here for the importance of adopting a sideways back-foot and upper body position. This is the only way to achieve lateral avoidance of the dangerous ball, because a front-on player will offer such a large target that he will have to duck into the line of the ball.

Obviously there is much more to batting than playing technique. I have no time to discuss the importance of experience, concentration, determination, relaxation, running between wickets, adaptation to conditions, placing and pacing the stroke etc, – not to mention adaptation from one-day play to five-day play and vice versa. I will just comment in passing that a requirement to score runs quickly is not entirely a new phenomenon in the history of the game.

Attitudes

I wish to make two other pleas before I close. The first is that the batsman, once assured of his technique, should be continuously encouraged and given as much confidence as possible. He is essentially a different animal from the bowler and the wicket-keeper – and should be treated as such.

Fear of getting out and fear of the ensuing public failure are the inhibiting factors. These should not be allowed to loom over-large in his mind. Most good players have had the confidence to play each ball on its merits, whatever the match position. On the other hand, getting out in a tight situation is often equated with lack of proper concern for the team, when in reality it is the tight situation which has uncovered a technical weakness.

Gentlemen, I believe you should play a more rigorous role in the training of young batsmen on first arrival at the county, or wherever potentially good players first appear. We should aim for a climate in which, like Jack Nicklaus in the golfing world, the best players look for guidance when things go wrong, thereby setting an example for the lesser lights to follow.

A sound basic technique is essential to good batting – Boycott is our only sideways player of the last decade, while every other known variation has been tried without conspicuous success. You, gentlemen, are the people to ensure that a larger pool of young batsmen will grow up in this game with good habits instilled into them, so that amongst them it will be more likely that we will find the two or three quality batsmen we need to rank beside Greg Chappell, Gavaskar and the two Richards.

ALL ROUNDERS

L. E. G. AMES
T. E. BAILEY
M. J. PROCTER

This short list should, of course, be headed by Gary Sobers, but his inordinate skills have spirited him higher into the legendary world. This is a book about batting and relatively normal all-rounders like Greig, Botham, Goddard, or Barlow cannot make the grade – not with the bat alone.

I have included Bailey because he made an unlikely batting style work to such good effect at the highest level and caused the bowlers such immense annoyance in the process. Procter comes in as one of the cleanest hitters of a cricket ball you would ever want to see with a style all of his own. Leslie Ames, the wicket-keeper batsman, simply made so many hundreds that he picked himself.

L E G AMES

ENGLAND

There are many reasons for including so great a cricketer as Ames and I will relate just a few. He is one of the few people with whom a discussion on cricket remains firmly based on fact not fiction, on opinion not prejudice. In passing I should mention that I was a keen supporter of my old colleague, Jim Parks, very much the batsman-wicket-keeper rather than the other way round, during that marvellous Sussex ball-player's successful time as England wicket-keeper.

As for Leslie Ames, I admire the man immensely, enjoy his company and would like to write something about him as a poor second best to seeing him play, which I was unfortunately too young to do. One thing was certain while Ames held his England place, and that was that the old argument as to whether the best wicket-keeper in the country was picked regardless of whether he could bat or not, just never arose. He proved himself one of the best batsmen and could command a place on that alone, apart from having no very serious rivals with the gloves on. When the selectors sat down there was always one name that could be inked in solid before discussions started – and that was Ames. It also gives me the opportunity to reveal that Dexter the all-rounder – batsman/medium-fast heretic bowler, kept wicket himself at junior colts level and was not entirely lacking in these skills. However, it did not take long for the scouting system among Radley College masters to wonder why an athletic (and for his age oversized) young man could bowl at a nifty speed in the nets and yet waste his time crouched behind the stumps when others available could clearly undertake the job just as well, if not better.

I wonder, though, how much that spell behind the wicket assisted me in learning how to bat. It is certainly a marvellous vantage point, unmatched by any other position on the field. A wicket-keeper with a cricketing brain can be of invaluable assistance to his captain, and to the bowlers, in planning a method of attack against a batsman, and if he doesn't learn something about

L E G AMES

One of cricket's immortals, Leslie Ames set the standard for all future wicket-keeper-batsmen. An example of his brilliant all-round ability was witnessed at Brentford in 1938 when Kent scored 803 for four, the highest total this century by a first-class county, and went on to beat Essex by an innings and 192 runs. Ames' contribution was 202 not out, and seven dismissals from behind the stumps. Note the 'weak' left hand grip and the angles of the head and shoulder showing no strain.

the art of batting after standing behind good players for hour after hour, then he must entirely lack the power to assimilate experience and knowledge.

Ames hardly falls into this category because I daresay there were more wicket-keepers who learned something about batting by standing behind Ames than vice versa. He was simply outstanding.

Consider the great wicket-keepers; most of them were not the best batsmen in the world but down in the order they often revealed stubborn (sometimes engaging and lively) qualities, and proved difficult to shift. There was Oldfield, Cameron, Duckworth, Strudwick, Levett, McIntyre, Tallon, Grout, Evans, Knott . . . it's a long list, even without Murray and Parks. But Leslie Ames must surely come top. Evans 'was the man who succeeded him as Kent's wicket-keeper, and no one could have faced a tougher assignment, for Ames has gone down in history as one of cricket's immortals. The greatest wicket-keeper-batsman the game has ever known'. Agreed, but certainly Evans kept the flame burning.

Contemporary accounts, as usual, do Ames' batting scant justice. In *Wisden* 1929, he is passed off as merely a 'pretty player'. 'Ames has a pretty style as a batsman and is not afraid to hit [the ball] hard.' However the critic was wise enough to qualify his remarks by ending 'and he may become the best wicket-keeper batsman that England has ever had.' A. G. Moyes makes the point that the Australians never saw him at his best. 'In Australia he was a wicket-keeper who might get runs, while in England he was in the first flight, resourceful where he had been hesitant, purposeful where he had been timid, driving with great power . . .'

Even more daunting and impressive is this: 'Ames [was] an orthodox, but free-scoring batsman who showed a fine full face of the bat during the operative part of the stroke. He was a particularly good hooker and cutter, and is the only wicket-keeper to have made a hundred centuries.' That was the late Ian Peebles. And the late Denzil Batchelor wrote: 'Wicket-keeper-batsman or batsman-wicket-keeper? That is, of course, the problem that Ames, Tallon and the late H. B. Cameron, among modern cricketers, seriously set us. In Ames's case I put him down as a batsman first. . .' And so it goes on and will provoke a lot of discussion and, no doubt, heated argument. One thing will never be disputed. He was a grand master of two crafts, and was once, I seem to recall, called 'an idle devil' because he didn't take up bowling!

LESLIE ETHELBERT GEORGE AMES CBE 1926–1951

Career Figures:	Innings 950	Runs 37,245	Average 43.56
Tests (47):	Innings 72	Runs 2,434	Average 40.56

T E BAILEY

ENGLAND

Certainly, Bailey is one of the great treasures and, indeed, 'entertainers' of English post-war cricket. He still goes on, writing and broadcasting about the game with a nice blend of judgement and authority; he may strike a pompous note from time to time but he never takes *himself* too seriously. Writing about himself, he is very good indeed.

'I sometimes wonder to what extent circumstances, and Test cricket in particular, were responsible for my becoming a stone-waller. Would I have been an entirely different player if I had been brought up in Kent where the pitches were normally good and encouraged stroke-making, or was there always an inclination towards the passive which had been merely subdued in my early days? I cannot really say, but I do remember P. G. Wodehouse coming down to Dulwich to watch a match against St Paul's, and writing an account for the magazine. I was at the crease for some time on that occasion without contributing many runs. P. G. Wodehouse summed things up beautifully: "Bailey awoke from an apparent coma to strike a boundary."'

The self-analysis goes on: 'Because of my pronounced initial forward movement it followed that I played a high percentage of fast bowling with my weight on my front foot. This meant I could never hook efficiently as I did not have sufficient time to move into the correct position. It also necessitated my learning how to "give" at the moment of contact when a ball suddenly lifts. This is an especially important technique on the untrustworthy pitch since it enables one to "drop" on the ball dead even when struck on the gloves.'

The other necessary skill which Bailey does not mention as a confirmed front foot player, was the ability to leave the ball which is just too wide on the off, lifting or possibly leaving the bat. This is the standard delivery to anyone who is coming forward before the ball is bowled. Obviously if you pitch on a length, bowling to hit the stumps, then the batsman is already at an advantage, since he is automatically playing the correct stroke. On the other hand

the forward push is normally quite wrong to the ball short of a length, especially if it is moving away to the slips. Perhaps because Bailey was so restricted in the alternatives contemplated to any given ball, that is he would expect to drop the majority dead at his feet, he still had the time and the ability to calculate when the danger ball should be left alone. Bailey has been rightly described as a genuine Test-class all-rounder, virtually the man for all seasons.

As one of my two all-rounders, the other being Procter – and you couldn't find two more different cricketers if you tried (a triumph for the theory that cricket can accommodate all sorts and conditions of men) – I must not forget to consider Bailey the bowler. I can easily forget his batting, almost every

T E BAILEY

Trevor Bailey, England's great all-rounder of the fifties, established a reputation for being a bit of a stone-waller. He is best known for his match-winning stand with Willie Watson in the England v Australia match at Lord's in 1953. He will also be remembered for his 68 runs in 458 minutes, scored against Australia at Brisbane on England's 1958/59 tour. In both photographs the bat is a long way out front, but the head positions are excellent.

single he played, except perhaps the Watson-Bailey affair at Lord's. However, I am as enthusiastic about his bowling as I am disparaging about his batting style. His was not a fluent action but it had everything needed for medium pace bowling of the highest class. Bailey was a real worker and thinker. He made himself bowl from very close to the stumps, often suffering knocks on the fingers from hitting them on his way through, bowled from his full height and kept his arm ramrod straight over the top. The result was an ability to move the ball both ways off the seam and in the air, like Derek Shackleton or Tom Cartwright, but that much quicker and with that extra life and bounce which made him Test match class.

'He was the first man to complete the double in 1949, whereafter in a span of ten years covering tours to Australia, West Indies, New Zealand and South Africa, he completed the unique performance of making 2,000 runs and taking 100 wickets in Test matches.'

Bailey lives in popular memory for his batting against Australia in the Lord's Test of 1953 (the Watson-Bailey affair) when, with defeat imminent, he stayed in with Willie Watson for most of the final day. This saved the game for England and provided the mainspring for the regaining of the Ashes after twenty years.

Whether as captain of Cambridge, Essex, or later, when automatic choice as England's top all-rounder, Bailey never failed to attract jeers for an alliance of slow-scoring and dedicated batting. It is intriguing that, as a man who never captained England and gained no conspicuous success as captain of Essex, he has subsequently been regarded as supreme among tacticians and technical analysts of the game. His reputation in this field has grown so much that in a relatively recent poll he was made an almost automatic choice to captain a team of the best post-war players. It may seem strange that this should be the popular view of Bailey, and it would be fascinating to find out if those selected would reach the same conclusion. For all Bailey's qualities of old, I wonder whether his stone-walling and characteristic inclination for negative tactics would have inspired ten other men to give of their best. He remains the England captain manqué.

TREVOR EDWARD BAILEY 1945–1967

Career Figures:	Innings 1072	Runs 28,642	Average 33.42
Tests (61):	Innings 91	Runs 2,290	Average 29.74

M J PROCTER

SOUTH AFRICA

Procter has such prodigious talent that it is hard to know in which of my somewhat vague categories to place him. Obviously he is an all-rounder of the highest class, but he could well go among the big hitters, certainly can keep company with some of the fastest scoring batsmen of all time, but could rest just as easily alongside the batting stylists.

He should, however, be included in any anthology of batsmen for one specific trait. That is the high ratio of boundaries to any other form of score, be it ones, twos or threes. Statistically there could be a number of reasons to account for such an imbalance. Unless you were to know otherwise, it could be that he was a very slow or indifferent runner between wickets, whereas the truth is very much the opposite. It could be that he was simply a slogger applying maximum power to every shot on a hit or miss basis. Neither of these possibilities is anywhere near the mark, and the truth lies nearer to straightforward technique and basic ability.

To illustrate this I can instance one short innings at The Oval, for the Rest of the World side under Gary Sobers when the first cancelled South African tour to England happened. There were already a fair number of runs on the board and clearly Procter's job was to push the score along. When he played an absolutely passive dead bat to the first few deliveries the bowler might have felt that he was to be let off lightly. With hardly more ado the next two balls went sizzling to the boundary, then that impassive block again, then two more crashing blows. Each ball was played strictly on its merits and the merest hint of a scoring opportunity was turned to immediate and maximum profit.

With some lesser players a tendency to wait and wait for the bad ball to hit for four is the worst possible contribution to an effective batting partnership with the man at the other end, especially when the said player, having waited for five balls, is desperate for a single off the sixth! No such criticism could

Although Mike Procter is one of the fastest-scoring batsmen of all time, he is no mere slogger of the ball. He has a straigthforward technique and plays each ball on its merits, making sure that few boundary-scoring opportunities are missed.

ever be levelled at Procter because he was never long in waiting for the ball that could turn into a boundary-scoring opportunity.

For this reason it must be said that his batting lacks a certain fluency which would typify an innings by Graveney, or Cowdrey perhaps. There is a certain staccato element, or should I say a hint, of the big drum being beaten from time to time rather than the more constant song of the violin. Such an analogy is, of course, altogether too disparaging. It would take a dedicated musician indeed to go to a concert to hear just the bass drummer, whereas Procter has always been high on my list of batsmen who were eminently worth watching. If I had the choice on any given day of watching either him or Barry Richards, I think I would probably settle the matter with the toss of a coin, and, of course, in their historical time and place they rank together.

Barry Richards writes: 'I first met Mike Procter in 1958 when he was at Primary School for under eleven years of age . . . We met again when we had both reached High School level, played together for the South African Schools side and came to England.' That is the background; then Procter and Richards were together in 1965 with Gloucestershire . . . 'We have both missed out on an extended Test match career because of the political situation in South Africa. We are both labelled as great players but it is hard to prove if you are not playing Test cricket.'

The tributes have fallen thick and fast: Brian Clough (football manager and cricket fan) rates Procter 'as one of the great players of my lifetime.' He was one of those batsmen who are also deadly and formidable in the bowling and fielding department. Here is Peter Pollock: 'The timing and sheer grace as the left foot moves forward, followed by a high backlift and a precision downswing, seems as effortless as a gazelle bounding through the open veldt. One would even assume that Mike could play a cover drive before he started walking . . . It is rather strange that Procter the bowler should be so much more unorthodox and that his batting, fielding, throwing and catching should ooze textbook method and charm.'

A shrewd aside – and possibly the best summing-up of the batsman-bowling dilemma, comes from Alan Gibson in *The Cricketer* 1973: 'Procter's development as a cricketer has been much influenced by Gloucestershire, because Gloucestershire in his time have needed a hundred wickets from him more than two thousand runs. In South Africa, where he scored his six successive centuries in 1970–71 (equalling the record of Fry and Bradman, though possibly in less taxing circumstances), he has always been able to do more justice to his batting. Even so, I have always felt that Gloucestershire put him in too high in the order. He has great strength, but he is mortal, and nobody can be expected to take all the wickets and score all the runs on seven days of a week.'

It has been suggested that, without denying Procter's great abilities, he is something of a slogger in the manner of the immortal Jessop. For example his longest innings of the summer of 1979 was 122 in one hundred and four minutes but, writes Christopher Coley in *Wisden Cricket Monthly*, 'nobody who has ever seen him bat could possibly suggest that his bat is anything but straight. His hitting in the air is deliberate and don't let us forget that when the ball is struck hard and high no fielder, Derek Randall included, can do very much about it. His favourite area is the arc between cover and dead straight – not an area where sloggers usually specialise . . . Yes, the great Gilbert Jessop himself, scorer of twelve hundreds in under an hour, acclaimed in *Wisden* as "the most exciting cricketer of them all", would have approved of Mike Procter's recent exploits. Rumour has it that Jessop scored his runs at the remarkable rate of 80 runs an hour. Well, in the last four matches of 1979 Procter actually exceeded this rate.'

An easy-going, unselfconscious character, Procter's effective presence on the cricket field is the perfect answer to those who claim that the modern game cannot be played successfully without a display of overt tension and pressure.

MICHAEL JOHN PROCTER 1965–

Career Record:	Innings 615	Runs 20,825	Average 37.12
Tests (7):	Innings 10	Runs 226	Average 25.11

ARTISTS

D. C. S. COMPTON
R. N. HARVEY
A. R. MORRIS
NAWAB OF PATAUDI
B. SUTCLIFFE
M. P. DONNELLY
F. M. M. WORRELL

I am told that there are concert pianists who have won acclaim more for their overall interpretation of the music than for the actual accuracy of their technique. Surely there is a close analogy here with Compton making a hundred at Lord's. Perfection was less important than invention and enjoyment. The ability to make the unorthodox seem attractive and dangerous sallies appear safe is what gives these men their special claim to immortality.

There are four left-handers, Harvey, Morris, Sutcliffe and Donnelly in the group which is perhaps no surprise. Batting this way round, these men had opportunities for stroke-play against right arm fast bowling denied to their right-handed counterparts. In a sense I am surprised there are not more 'lefties', but these four have their place because they had the wit as well as the skill to make use of their advantage. They certainly sent thrills down the backs of spectators in the process.

Pataudi's footwork was an art in itself and just one late cut by Frank Worrell was surely the equivalent of any single brush stroke, oil on canvas, by an old master.

I am sad to find that the likes of Zaheer Abbas and Asif Iqbal have not had their due in these pages, although this category would be right for them if there was the time and space.

Imagination, a certain carefree attitude and a vast talent is the requirement for a place in this section and I hope I have done justice to these qualities in the chosen few.

D C S COMPTON

ENGLAND

The first-class career of Denis Compton and of Edward Dexter just overlapped and my only memory is playing against Denis for the Gentlemen against the Players at Lord's, one of the last such matches to take place. It is not surprising that I should remember that game because, in a mixed bowling career, it remains a highlight as I took eight wickets in the match and had an analysis of five wickets for only eight runs in the first innings – a performance I am allowed to cherish and remember, in that a ball was presented to me after the game, with a silver plaque suitably inscribed.

One of the victims (or should I say two) was in fact Denis Compton, although he was towards the end of his career and I was at the beginning of mine. But it was certainly not so much my skill as a bowler as the lively state of the pitch which accounted for Compton falling foul of such raw talent twice in one match.

Many years before as a schoolboy, I had fleetingly met the great man, when I was sitting on the grass by the boundary rope at Lord's for a Test match between England and South Africa (when Bill Edrich took Dudley Nourse's middle stump out of the ground in the first over of the day – in fact I'm not sure that it wasn't the first ball). Denis was fielding on the boundary and he must have been the first famous cricketer whose autograph I dared solicit. I may say that he turned me down with his usual charm, saying that if he gave an autograph to me then he would have to oblige all the other children.

So my first encounters gave me no inkling of the genius which he was universally accorded. I know for a fact, however, that he was indeed a genius at striking the cricket ball with the bat. Indeed, I once saw him as an ageing gentleman in his mid-fifties, corpulent and suffering badly with his feet and back (Denis Compton has been prey to gout from time to time); he had certainly had no practice within weeks of the match and he had certainly no knock-up. Nevertheless, he walked out to bat with his usual jaunty stride, took guard and started to walk towards the oncoming bowler for his very first ball and proceeded to strike a straight one clean out of the ground with his very first hit. Co-ordination of hand and eye was, therefore, in perfect tune, in perfect harmony without any of the normal preparations. If that isn't genius, I wonder what is.

What further can be said about Denis Charles Scott Compton CBE, born in 1918, that has not been said before? Well, one might turn to that master of English prose and cricketing insight, R. C. Robertson-Glasgow, in *Cricket Prints*. This terse and witty stuff makes your hair stand on end. 'Crusoe' had a leisurely impatience but he never wasted time: 'Enjoyment, given and felt, is the chief thing about Compton's batting. It has an easy freshness which the formality of the first-class game has not injured. It is a clear-flowing stream; a breath of half-holiday among work days. When he was still at an elementary school he made a century in a boy's match at Lord's. Sir Pelham Warner noted the omens. A spotter in another game had seen him, too, and Arsenal's Mr Allison summoned him to Highbury.'

There was more to come: 'Crusoe' again: 'Compton began with Middlesex in 1936, and in that season scored 1,004 runs. In 1937, just turned nineteen, he fell short of 2,000 by only 20 runs . . . Purists noted that his left leg wasn't always near the bat during the off-drive, but the ball kept hitting the boundary all the same. More interesting was his bold attack against slow bowling. No one so nimble yet powerful had been seen since Hammond first began. He played in all four Tests against Australia in 1938 and began with a century in the first Test at Nottingham . . . In temperament Compton is confident and equable. Nature and environment have been very good to him. Set fair for greatness.'

Well, we have to settle for that. 'Set fair for greatness' indeed. 'Crusoe' was bang on; the launching of Compton was to result in a not always settled but certainly superb vintage. What an intuitive genius. I have often wondered if this superbly gifted cricketer was conscious of what he was doing. Certainly for my own part, I might drift off, whether at the crease or in the field, and was often rebuked for so doing. I can only say that if you're any good at all (and you are what you are) it's not a bad habit. There is a certain state of trance in batting with determination, but without 'thinking' – when the first-class batsman with innate co-ordination never puts a foot wrong, simply because his feet are always in the right place. There is, of course, the other situation when you have to 'think' fiercely, keep your head down and stay in for hours. Players such as Bradman, Hammond, Compton and Sobers have always understood this; all that is required is the knack of staying in and scoring a lot of runs. In the end you must look at the averages. There was never a great batsman who got out early all the time.

My own judgement on Compton's style of play is that he was a superb

The old and the new. Denis Compton, yet to embark on his considerable Test career, walks to the wicket with the old campaigner E. H. Hendren during a match between Surrey and Middlesex in 1936.

watcher of the ball. He was predominantly a back foot player, and, in fact, had excellent footwork, blade work, and body positioning as well. He wasn't particularly fluent in the stroke – not a real swinger of the bat, more a stroker than a striker, and that accounts, I suppose, for his beautiful square driving and sweeping of the ball. But then almost all the very best players have been predominantly back foot, going out to drive only when the ball is well up, so that puts Denis in the common mould – or should I say, the common high-class mould?

But there are moments of crisis: at a certain stage in a cricketer's career he may feel that the roof has fallen in, that the skill has deserted him, and that the bloom has gone for good. After the war, back in England from India, Compton in his book *End of an Innings* writes: 'I didn't start well . . . I had a spell from late May when in six county innings and a Test match innings I had scores of 10, 0, 7, 0, 8, 0 and 1: a total of 26 runs in seven innings. For the first time I lost all my confidence, more totally than I was ever to lose it again . . . The climax was at Lord's, on my own ground, in my first post-war Test [against India].' He was bowled first ball – the shortest of all stays at the crease.

But soon the tide turned, in most dramatic fashion. It was against Warwickshire at the end of June – and at Lord's again. 'I went out to the wicket hardly knowing which end of the bat to hold, and with my confidence absolutely nil, to a delivery from Hollies [that man again] I tried to play what I thought was a correct stroke, edged the ball, and, with a strange kind of fascination, saw it roll gently onto the wicket . . . the ball touched the stumps all right and the bails shook, but didn't fall . . . After that I decided to throw the bat at the ball. I did so to the next delivery, made contact beautifully and saw it go sailing into the Grandstand balcony. I went on to make 122 and at the end of the innings I was a man with confidence in himself full restored.'

In 1946 Compton, at the age of twenty-six, went with MCC to Australia. It was not too happy an occasion. Hammond was over the hill but Bradman wasn't. And two 'very formidable customers called Lindwall and Miller' were approaching their prime. But it was in England, in 1947, after a cruel winter which was succeeded by an everlasting summer, that Compton's genius flowered with the help of another great player – Bill Edrich. 'The Middlesex Twins' gave the counties some awful stick. Compton made tons of runs, all with the same bat. 'It was a light bat, about two pounds and two ounces, with a short handle . . . also it had a narrow grain, which is not supposed to last well, though the drive in it is usually better. This one drove beautifully from the beginning, and lasted the whole season . . . I acquired it from Warsops, whose managing director, George Hunt, recommended it to me at the opening of the 1947 season.'

In 1948 it was a different matter. It was Bradman's swansong, but he

Predominantly a back-foot player of the ball, Denis Compton was one of the finest batsmen to grace England's cricket fields. His innate co-ordination, and perfect temperament, raised him to the class of 'artist' among batsmen. He was, indeed, a 'breath of half-holiday among work days'.

brought with him Lindwall, Miller, Johnston, Johnson and Toshack. It was difficult to cope with that lot. At Nottingham, Compton recalls, 'Hutton was hit on a number of occasions but I managed, I remember, to get out of the way. Before very long I became conscious of Bradman at cover-point, grinning his head off . . . When we were leaving the field at the close of play I walked alongside him: "Well, Don, I saw you enjoying yourself just now . . ." He wasn't smiling any more. "You've got a bat in your hand, haven't you? You should be able to get out of the way. I used to love it when I played against bouncers. I used to hook them." I don't remember any more of the conversation. And I don't remember Bradman, the target of the bouncers in the thirties, ever before having expressed such tolerant and amiable views on the matter.'

Meanwhile Compton went on, getting more and more unfit (his famous knee), and yet, strangely, better and better – witness his innings at The Oval when he made the winning hit and England regained the Ashes against Hassett's side in 1953. It was not so long after this that I was to meet Denis in another role (it's funny how our paths have crossed from time to time in life without getting together much on the cricket field).

It was Denis who introduced me to my first and only agent, Bagenal Harvey. It was the start of a long business relationship, in that Harvey even now negotiates my television and newspaper contracts and a certain amount of other engagements as well. I like to think that Denis Compton had, in fact, picked me out as a likely lad from the younger brigade, and, if he had, if he wasn't simply playing the field, perhaps he can congratulate himself on picking out somebody who did reasonably well.

Subsequently, I have had many a gay (original usage) day in the Press Box trying to pick a winner and watching the odd race on television to prove which of us was the better tipster. Of course, the only abiding problem with Denis is his timekeeping. He never wears a watch and insists from year to year that he has turned over a new leaf. He now keeps an effective diary and attempts never to say that he will be somewhere where he isn't. But the fact remains that at crucial moments it is still a toss up whether Denis will show up on time. He will cheerfully turn up one hour late, or appear a month from now, with an affable smile, but without even an explanation or a touch of conscience that he wasn't where he was supposed to be.

John Arlott recalls: 'Like Sobers, Denis Compton was one of the great *instinctive* cricketers, one of the greatest of all time . . . He differed from Len Hutton, his contemporary in the English side, in just about every way, and yet both were among the finest batsmen this country has ever produced. He did not rely, like Hutton, on perfect balance but on razor-sharp reflexes and a gift for improvisation which was quite marvellous to see . . . and he was the *cheekiest* batsman I ever saw.'

In 1957, Compton played his last first-class innings (at Lord's for Middlesex). In the first innings he was dropped at three and then went on to make a century – very typical of the man. In *The World of Cricket* there is a snooty but noble tribute: 'Denis Compton, as one of the greatest artists the game has known, made a strangely plebian start by being born in Hendon. He should, in the light of future events, have been borne down from Valhalla on a silver cloud.' Enough said.

DENIS CHARLES SCOTT COMPTON CBE 1936–1964

Career Figures:	Innings 839	Runs 38,942	Average 51.85
Tests (78):	Innings 131	Runs 5,807	Average 50.06

R N HARVEY

AUSTRALIA

Before discussing the merits of this brilliant Australian cricketer I had better clear the air by recalling an incident during the England tour of Australia in 1962–63. I was the England captain, Benaud captained Australia, and Neil Harvey was his vice-captain. When the tour was over, I had dinner with Harvey, his wife and Benaud. It had been a tough and grinding series, but there were hard men on both sides. Jack Fingleton wrote of the final Test at Sydney: 'If the road to hell is paved with good intentions, as we are told, then let the road to Sydney not only be paved with the intentions of the whole summer but indeed consummated with them . . . a cricket tour we all want to forget.'

At the dinner with Harvey, who had announced his retirement, I listened to his plans for a new commercial venture. A few days later he attacked me (in the press) at some length and in extraordinary fashion. He wrote: '[he was] the worst England captain I have met . . . seldom have I seen a prominent visitor to this country appear to be at times so ungracious to his hosts, the Australian team.'

Well now, that must be good for a chuckle! And it looks good on paper: 'his hosts, the Australian team'. But can committed opponents on the field suddenly switch to the role of host and guest when the umpires remove the bails each evening? I don't think so. Obviously there will be individual friendships which spring up. There are even token visits for a beer from one dressing room to the other. But the visiting team is the guest of the Board of Control – not of the opposing players. So, if in the hurly burly of the Test series I was less than gracious to Mr Harvey as an individual, it would have been a personal matter rather than some diplomatic failing on my part. Harvey and I were of different generations in any case, and unlikely to be overnight pals. Anyway it was I who made friendly conversation over dinner and Harvey who gave me a hard time in the press. But never mind, it was too long ago to worry about and he and I can pass the time of day together now without animosity.

Now for Harvey the cricketer. Born in 1928, he played for Australia, Victoria, and New South Wales and has been described, precisely, 'as left-handed, small and nimble . . . and his fielding, developed at baseball, was exceptional'. Again, from another source: 'In fifteen years, between 1948 and 1963, Harvey played in more Test matches than any other Australian, scored more runs in Tests than all but Sir Donald Bradman, and was headed by only that great batsman in Australian Test centuries . . . Like most who have possessed beautiful footwork at the batting crease Harvey was small of stature, but there was nothing small about his batting.' As for his fielding – whether in the covers, boundary or the slips – the same artistry and technical finesse was apparent: 'small and dapper, swooping on the ball and flicking it back to the wicket-keeper with a minimum of effort, inches from the top of the bails.' Yes, batting apart, he was a danger-man in the field – shades of Davidson, Colin Bland and Clive Lloyd.

Harvey's book *My World of Cricket* has some good moments but has a slightly peevish tone: 'When Ian Johnson retired from the game on his return from England after the 1956 tour I thought I had as good a chance as anyone to take over the reins of leadership of my country. My batting record since reaching Test class had been the best of any Australian batsman and I really felt I had earned the captaincy. But as history shows, things didn't work out and the Australian Board of Control preferred firstly Ian Craig then Richie Benaud. . . '

One must tread carefully in these matters. Lord knows there were many people who thought I should never have been appointed captain of England. But with all respect to Harvey, I think the Australian selectors were right. Benaud (as I found to my cost from time to time) proved to be a captain of the highest class – always plotting, thinking, on the prowl, as hard as iron; he just wanted to win all the time. Harvey the left-hander is a curious case. He writes: 'I am not a natural left-hander and I can think of no valid reason why I bat that way except that the first time I picked up a cricket bat it seemed more comfortable to grip it with my left hand at the bottom of the handle. . . I do only three things with my left hand – bat, play golf and chop wood. In all other respects I am right-handed – I play tennis, billiards, squash, throw the ball and write my letters that way.' There were six cricketers in the Harvey family – all right-handers. Sensibly, none of them put pressure on Neil to change his style.

This left-handed business (and not only in cricket) deserves a book on its own. At Adelaide, in 1955, Len Hutton was batting against Alan Davidson and Ian Johnson. 'Hutton', writes Harvey, 'complained to the umpire about Davidson's follow-through. . . I passed Hutton at the end of the over and

Australia's second highest scorer of all time, Neil Harvey was a ferocious player of the off-drive. He was also a superb fielder, first at cover point and then in the slips.

asked him what he was making a fuss about. . . When he told me he was concerned about Davidson digging up the pitch, I replied:"You ought to turn round and bat left-handed and see how tough the rough is then." Hutton had no answer to that.'

I would have had an answer: 'OK, the rough may cause trouble with a spin bowler against you but what about the advantage of the left-hander in having the great majority of fast and medium fast bowling coming from right-handers bowling over the wicket?'

Now some right hand batsmen, some very great ones, including Geoff Boycott, never effectively adapt their technique to cope with the occasional left arm, fast bowler. Sobers, Solkar, Dymock and many others have all given Boycott infinitely more trouble than any right-handers. Personally, I used to love playing Sobers, Davidson and the lesser lights though they obviously had their successes against me.

The reason is relatively simple but it's a technical matter which relates to the lbw law. When a left arm bowler dropped the ball short to me, I knew that it was almost certainly pitched outside the leg stump – therefore I could not be lbw. I could play back and look to pull or hook the ball with impunity. The same length ball from right arm over the wicket is infinitely more dangerous because it may not bounce above stump high, and the pull or hook shot is fraught with danger unless the bounce is very consistent.

The other advantage is the freedom of stroke available when the ball pitches round off stump and a little wider. Again, the ball pitching in the same place from right arm over the wicket, is usually angled in towards the batsman's body and, as we say, 'tucks him up'. There is obviously a danger of a catch to the keeper or to the slips from this extra freedom; but I am in no doubt that the opportunities for stroke play are considerably greater when playing these left-handed angles as opposed to those set up by the mass of predominantly right handed bowlers. So the left-hander, faced with a preponderance of right-handed bowlers seems to me to enjoy a considerable advantage if only in the likely speed of his scoring.

Perhaps it was Harvey's fear of the rough outside his off stump which made him so nimble on his feet when playing spinners. Of all those I have seen, he ventured further down the pitch than anyone, and could mostly reach the ball on the full pitch, and only if he couldn't get that far did he need to play it back.

There was a memorable innings in this vein against England at Headingley on a broken pitch when Australia always looked to be losing. Harvey scored 73 out of 237 in the first innings and 53 out of 120 in the second innings. The slow bowlers against him were Tony Lock, who took only two wickets in 39 overs for exactly a hundred runs, and David Allen with three wickets for 75 in 42 overs. Their comparative lack of success on a broken pitch could be largely attributed to Harvey's mastery of conditions totally foreign to most Australians. But in Australia Harvey simply murdered Lock and Laker at Melbourne in the 1958–59 tour – there was no holding him.

I must end with a generous tribute from A. G. Moyes: 'Harvey created a pile of figures by stroke-making which was varied, fluent, powerful, and artistic. He was a batsman, not merely a gatherer of runs . . . he may easily rank among the immortals both as batsman and fieldsman.'

ROBERT NEIL HARVEY MBE 1946–1962

Career Figures:	Innings 461	Runs 21,699	Average 50.92
Tests (79):	Innings 137	Runs 6,149	Average 48.41

A R MORRIS

AUSTRALIA

As new generations come along and demand the day's newspaper headlines, it is as easy to forget how good past players were as it is to sing their praises. So a brief bit of homework about this engaging man is illuminating. Morris played for New South Wales and Australia. 'He was unchallenged from 1946 to 1955 as Australia's opening batsman. Left-handed, and displaying superb foot work against slow bowling, he headed the averages for Bradman's undefeated 1948 side in England, and altogether made eight centuries against England.' Another source says that 'he would sidle yards down the pitch to disturb the bowler's length.'

'The most triumphal of his seasons was that 1948 one in England where he was in command against bowlers of all types and paces. When Laker was found wanting at Headingley [in 1948, not 1956], it was Morris who led the second innings onslaught on him after Harvey, in the first, had put together his first century against England. In the Australian second innings Morris (182) and Bradman (173 not out) drove Australia to a remarkable victory which clinched the rubber . . .'

In 1963, eight years after retirement, Morris went on a short Commonwealth tour of India and South Africa, and his batting at Bombay was so magnificent that Indian players found themselves applauding his commanding stroke play. Norman O'Neill, himself no mean stroke player when in the mood, raced into the dressing room on this occasion to retrieve two other Australians who were resting: 'Come and watch this . . . you'll never see a better batsman than this fellow.'

Morris was one of those players you only needed to watch for half-an-hour to know you were in the presence of an exceptional talent. If he had not made his mark in that time, the likelihood was that he was already out and back in the pavilion. For him there were few days indeed when he found it necessary to scratch around for hours at a time while confidence and touch returned. Either the Morris system was working or it wasn't. The only time I saw him, I had the dubious distinction of bowling to him and he proceeded to dispatch my offerings to every part of the ground with the least possible effort and the maximum of bonhomie. Anyone who still thinks that all Australians are rough and ready, beer-drinking Pommie bashers, should meet the likes of Arthur Morris, who is quietly spoken and companionable. He always looked as though he enjoyed scoring runs against whatever county or country he played. Which is not to say he did not also enjoy the occasional glass of an appropriately comforting liquid.

In retrospect, it is as easy to forget bad times as well as good, and in Arthur Morris's life there was a bowler called Alec Bedser, who loomed large. Normally a right arm, over the wicket, inswing bowler against a quality left-handed batsman is not much of a contest. I remember the powerful Bob Barber dealing out some of the severest treatment to just such an honest toiler in the Johannesburg Test at The Wanderers Ground on the 1964–65

One of only two cricketers in the world to score a century in both innings on his debut in first-class cricket (the other being N. J. Contractor), the left-handed Arthur Morris fulfilled all expectations and became Australia's regular opening batsman between 1946 and 1955. In both this photograph and the photograph on page 45, his fine sense of balance is well in evidence.

tour. If the poor man bowled it straight he was clipped away on the leg side and every time he allowed it to swing then it got the full treatment through the covers. There seemed no refuge for the bowler, the captain, or the fielders until the unequal contest was interrupted by a change of bowling.

Alec Bedser was, of course, no ordinary inswing bowler because he could make the ball go the other way off the seam, and also he could genuinely spin the ball from leg off his mighty middle finger. He would get Morris going across too far with the late swing and then get him out with the ball that suddenly straightened.

For an on the spot report read Denzil Batchelor (a sort of dying fall with a triumphant ending): 'Morris found Bedser too much for him in the early Test against Brown's team . . . In three games running he returned to the pavilion hanging his pink head and golden curls over minute scores. Then the Fourth Test brought revenge: a double century, succulent and superb, reminded the world that . . . the handsomest left-hand bat is in the game today – and probably tomorrow.'

I must go back to Morris's innings at Headingley in 1948. Jim Swanton wrote: 'Morris's innings gives another lift to a reputation which has soared amazingly since it seemed even doubtful whether he might make the team for the first Test at Nottingham less that two months ago. Technically, he is wonderfully sound, with a supreme watchfulness and a knack of playing every stroke when beautifully balanced. But with great batsmen, and Morris now deserves to be ranked in that small, illustrious army, a temperament is even more than technique . . .'

Swanton also wrote: 'It was a nice point in the first years after the war whether Arthur Morris, Martin Donnelly, or Bert Sutcliffe was the best left-handed batsman playing.' John Arlott, poet, football and cricket writer and commentator, hymn-writer, and wine connoisseur, collector of fine glass and good books, thinks that Martin Donnelly was the head lad in this department. Perhaps he was. As Swanton wrote in 1949: 'Hadlee batted with characteristic soundness, and if Donnelly made a few mistakes when the whole burden of the scoring fell upon him, his first 23 in a quarter of an hour was the gem of the day.'

There is no absolute answer when comparing great players – which is just as well! I can only think it is a matter of time and taste, of style and opposition.

ARTHUR ROBERT MORRIS MBE 1940–1964

Career Figures:	Innings 250	Runs 12,614	Average 53.67
Tests (46):	Innings 79	Runs 3,533	Average 46.48

A R MORRIS

NAWAB OF PATAUDI

INDIA

I must begin by eliminating confusion. This piece is about the Nawab of Pataudi, junior. But he followed in the footsteps of his father, the Nawab of Pataudi, senior, (1910–1952), who played both for England and India in a Test Match. Pataudi senior is described in *The World of Cricket* as 'a player of great gifts, quick to sight the ball and to move his feet, but his fluent stroke play had a firm basis alike in judicious patience and basically correct technique. He died of a heart attack when in the saddle playing polo.'

The son, born in 1941, captained Winchester, Oxford, Sussex, and India. In 1961 he was a passenger in a car crash, and collided with the windscreen. He hurt his shoulder and his hand, and a splinter of glass entered his right eye. Pataudi, in his book *Tiger's Tale* writes: 'You will find it better to play cricket using only one eye.' This was the verdict of a distinguished eye specialist, Sir Benjamin Rycroft. 'It took me a long time to realise that I had virtually lost the use of one eye, but even then, never for an instant did I consider I might not be able to play cricket again.'

Courage and determination apart, some technical adjustments were imperative. 'At first I couldn't pick the length of the bowling at all. Then I reached a sort of compromise, but I suppose it took five years before I could claim to be completely on terms with my handicap.'

Coming to terms with a handicap is a far cry from overcoming it. To have completely recaptured the mastery of his younger days would have been an achievement indeed, and, even though Pataudi went on to score Test hundreds with monocular sight, they were ususally patient affairs, bringing all his experience to bear, experience gained while he had the full sight of two very keen eyes.

While fully sighted, Pataudi had been a prodigy indeed. As a schoolboy he had made mock of the best bowling set against him, and as his reputation grew, he dismissed the best club attacks that could be mounted against him. Then at University he stepped onto a new plateau of excellence, quickly learning the new lessons imposed by professional bowlers of both second and first elevens, until he made sport for his own pleasure with their offerings also. In one season he strung a number of consecutive centuries together and thereby proved himself one of the very few sons of famous fathers about whom it cannot be said, 'He'll never be as good as his dad.'

Then his turn came for Sussex. This time the only adjustments he had to make to meet better bowling standards came during the usual breaking-in period on which the older professionals insist so that the up and coming youngster knows his place and is restrained from putting on too many airs. Pataudi's settling-in period was a great deal shorter than most, and soon he was helping his county to championship victories with the same vigour and audacity that had marked his play from the early days at Winchester.

Pataudi was naturally keen and quick in everything he did, and this was the hallmark of his batting, accompanied by fleet-footed running between the wickets. He and Asif Iqbal would have been some partnership in a limited-overs match because if any combination could have turned one run into two it would have been this one. Then there was his stroke-making off both front foot and back foot, with the bat equally at home in the horizontal as in the vertical plane.

It was a major loss to the history of the game that these skills should not have flowered to full maturity at the highest level – and all because of a split-second miscalculation in a motor car. There was every reason to believe that the development of his ability through the various levels of the game would have continued unabated at Test level, where dominating innings of the Bradman or Sobers ilk could naturally have been expected. If anyone wants proof of that he need only look at Pataudi's Test record when all but sightless in the injured eye. I have tried batting with one eye closed and, although it is by no means impossible, it certainly approximates to playing snooker without the forward hand to steady the cue. Presumably there is an increase in the power of the remaining eye, and further development of the senses to compensate for what is missing, but Pataudi's performance remains unique.

He went back home to India. Then he was asked to captain the President's eleven against MCC at Hyderabad. I was the other captain. Pataudi recalls: 'After completing the toss, Ted Dexter and I were strolling together back to the pavilion when he asked me "Well, Tiger what are you going to do?" "No, Ted," I replied, "what are *you* going to do?" I then continued, "Look here, you won the toss didn't you?"'

Well, no, I hadn't won the toss and, unlike the other time this embarrassing contretemps happened to me, in Perth, I was sure of my ground. Pataudi elected to bat and for him it was a harrowing experience. He writes: 'For my own moment of trial I decided to wear a contact lens in my right eye. To my discomfort I found I was seeing two balls, six to seven inches apart. By

Few batsmen could beat the speed of the Nawab of Pataudi between the wickets, but even his natural elegance was ruffled occasionally. A cricketing child prodigy, the Nawab tragically lost the sight of one eye at an early age. Undeterred, he went on to enjoy a distinguished career for Sussex and India.

picking the inner one I managed to score thirty-five runs before tea. Then I removed the contact lens and, keeping the bad eye closed, completed top score of seventy before being caught by Ken Barrington off the bowling of Tony Brown.'

Fate had certainly chosen the 'right' eye: had the left eye been so damaged it would probably have ended Pataudi's cricketing career. At Madras he gave us a thrashing, making 103 in two hours twenty minutes. Then in 1964, at the same ground, he made 128 not out against Australia; and 148 at Headingly in 1967. 'Tiger, tiger, burning bright.'

Sussex have had some eminent captains in their time – Ranjitsinhji, C. B. Fry, Gilligan, Duleepsinhji, S. C. Griffith, Barlett, Langridge, Sheppard, Doggart, Marlar, and – after me in 1966 – Pataudi. But as he reflects, with feeling, 'I couldn't see myself playing county cricket for a whole season, six days a week. That is too much of a good thing, enough to make even the keenest player stale and bored at some stage.' Yes indeed. The time came when I knew that I had shot my bolt. Stand down before it is too late and you have lost your edge. Let someone else have a go.

Let Pataudi have the last word on his own character and approach to the game: 'In the country of the blind, the one-eyed man is king. But in the keen-eyed world of cricket a fellow with just one good eye-and-a-bit has to settle for something less than the perfection he once sought. Lucky me, despite this, to have been able to play the game all over the world in the company of giants.'

NAWAB OF PATAUDI 1957–1976
(now Mansur Ali Khan)

Career Figures:	Innings 500	Runs 15,425	Average 33.60
Tests (46):	Innings 83	Runs 2,793	Average 34.91

B SUTCLIFFE
M P DONNELLY

NEW ZEALAND

It seems a good idea to put the two New Zealand left-handers together, so here they are in the same piece. Martin Donnelly was a bit older (born 1917) than Bert Sutcliffe, and may have stamped the pattern. C. B. Fry, asked which of the left-handers of his day he would rate superior to Martin Donnelly, replied unhesitatingly 'not one'.

Donnelly had toured England in 1937. In 1945 he scored a century at Lord's for Dominions v England. He then went to Oxford and flayed the opposition in the Parks. His 1946 century against Cambridge is recorded as one of the greatest innings in a Varsity match. The following year he made 162 for the Gentlemen, and in 1949 put the flourish on the top of the column in the Lord's Test when he made 206 for New Zealand.

His Oxford days inspired (perhaps even over-stimulated) the enthusiasm of the critics: 'Bare figures can give no idea of the electric atmosphere in the Parks when that short, sturdy figure went in to bat. A lucky spectator might have half an hour to spare between, say, a lecture at Keble and a tutorial in Parks Road. In that half-hour, he might well see Donnelly hit nine boundaries, each from a different stroke. Most exquisite of all would be the late cut and the straight drive; there would be an on-drive, a square leg-hit, a devastating hook, perhaps a rustic pull worthy of George Hirst.' And Donnelly is rated as one of the great cover points of all time: 'He was equally brilliant in anticipation, in pick-up and in throw . . . His cricket career was short: memories of it will endure.'

Sutcliffe (Bert) from New Zealand must not be confused with Sutcliffe (Herbert) the cricketer for Yorkshire and England. Bert is reckoned to be one of the best left-handed batsmen in the history of the game, and has made more runs and centuries than any other New Zealander. Further, he has been called 'one of the most productive and cultured batsmen in New Zealand's history . . . his left-handed stroke play has been characterised by adventure and artistry. He burst into prominence with scores of 197 and 128 in the same match against MCC at Dunedin in 1946–47, and thereafter his record flowered into magnificence'. Another great batsman condemned to become a captain.

Fred Trueman had this to say: 'Like all top-class openers he was nimble, with brilliant foot work, and it was perhaps unfortunate for him that he played for New Zealand when they were something of a Cinderella among Test-playing countries. It is never as easy to score runs in a struggling side, no matter how great one's ability . . .'

Then Denzil Batchelor added his comments: 'The first time I saw Bert Sutcliffe bat was at a net at Lord's before the 1949 New Zealand tour got under way . . . As the left-handed Viking, standing up straighter than is the custom, lambasted the bowlers about the Nursery Ground, Patsy Hendren beside me broke silence: "Two thousand five hundred runs," he said firmly, "two thousand five hundred runs in a season if ever I saw them." This

Bert Sutcliffe was one of the best left-handers in the game. Technically correct in all facets of batting, he was a graceful stroke-player and used to breach the gaps in the field with absolute precision.

unequivocal and pinpointing prophecy turned out to be exactly 127 runs short of the truth.'

Bert Sutcliffe's career may be divided into two: the first before he was hit a severe blow on the head in South Africa; and the second after that. I saw him play before that unhappy incident, but I only played against him afterwards, and it was a crying shame to see the difference. Nobody had stood taller and played the fast bowlers with more skill and courage. In fact I would go so far as to say that Sutcliffe's command of all the strokes, each one under perfect control, was the equal of any in this book.

Then came that fateful blow, and from that day on it was painful to watch this once great player flinching fractionally every time the ball came up around chest high. I remember reading that a terrifying flinch test was devised on aircraft carriers when pilots had been through a worse kind of hell in the Second World War. Massive hydraulic rams were used either in the launching of or in the arresting of the planes, and the test was to face up to within an inch of where the ram would come to a hurtling stop without drawing back. Whether this was a true test of nerves or simply a ghoulish form of amusement is immaterial. It was certainly not amusing to those who love the game of cricket, and to those who admire the people who play it best, to see Sutcliffe suffer. That he went on playing Test cricket at all is testimony enough to his spirit, but he was only a pale shadow of his former self.

Yet, if I had to pick a model left-hander for a young player to emulate, it would be Bert Sutcliffe. He was a balanced and neat good timer, a hard enough hitter with a complete range of strokes, good footwork, and splendid poise throughout. I have written of the most unfortunate accident off the field befalling Pataudi. No more was it Sutcliffe's fault that on the field a rogue delivery should catch him in two minds and involuntarily leave him with a split mind when facing similar bowling.

MARTIN PATERSON DONNELLY 1937–1961

Career Figures:	Innings	221	Runs	9,250	Average 47.43
Tests (7):	Innings	12	Runs	582	Average 52.90

BERT SUTCLIFFE 1941–1966

Career Figures:	Innings	405	Runs	17,283	Average 47.22
Tests (42):	Innings	76	Runs	2,727	Average 40.10

F M M WORRELL

WEST INDIES

Frank Worrell was probably just passing his peak when I first laid eyes on him. He was walking out to bat at Fenners, the immaculate Cambridge ground, playing for the West Indians against our motley crew of undergraduates. His record was already exceptional and we all knew him for a talented stroke player. What made the most impression, however, was not his play but the way he looked. He still remains for me the epitome of the well-dressed cricketer, and, as he walked out that sunny day with beautifully pressed, immaculately clean and crisp clothing, the colour of his skin contrasting so much with the clothes, there was already so much to admire, before he even took a ball. It was not only his clothes but his boots with brand new laces, apparently spanking new gloves, and bat, and pads, or, if they were not new, then certainly beautifully prepared for even this minor occasion in his cricketing life. It is in keeping with this memory that the number of runs he scored on that occasion has slipped away entirely.

In *Playfair Cricket Monthly* (May 1964), the editor, Gordon Ross, wrote an eloquent tribute to Sir Frank Worrell who had died the month before at the age of forty-three. Ross wrote of him as 'cricketer supreme, a wonderful ambassador for his native West Indies, and, to those of us who subsequently knew him and worked with him in press boxes on the cricket fields of England, the perfect gentleman . . . His contribution to the game of cricket and his ability to give West Indies belief in themselves and confidence to face the world on level terms, will remain his permanent memorial.'

In the same article there is a quote from Trevor Bailey, a specifically technical analysis: 'Tall and loosely built, he possessed a smoothness of movement and a feline grace which made him fascinating to watch, whether batting, bowling, or fielding . . . His back lift was high and preceded a full follow-through. Although he hit the ball very hard, he rather gave the impression of stroking it . . . There was poetry in his batting. I especially remember one stroke he made against Alec Bedser in a Test match at

Knighted for his services to West Indian cricket, Sir Frank Worrell displayed an artistry in his batting which few could emulate. Equally good off front and back foot, he was a fine cutter square of the wicket and a masterly player of slow bowling of all kinds.

Lord's. For once the "Big Fella" bowled a full half volley outside the off stump and Worrell immediately pounced upon this unexpected offering. Many players would have scored four off that delivery, but very few would have had the ability, or the instinct to reach the boundary *via* an exquisite late cut. This was West Indian magic and vintage Worrell.'

Obviously he had to be something special because he was an equal member of the famous trio, Weekes, Walcott and Worrell, and the exploits of the other two hit the cricketing headlines sufficiently to make that high praise indeed.

I have said that he was passing his peak when I first played against him, yet I was still to spend many hours in the field while he was amassing 197 in Barbados in January 1960 during the first Test match of the series when England toured under Peter May. Hardly a batsman over the top when you consider a stand with Sobers from 4.50pm on the Friday until 11.40am on the Tuesday – a total of nine hours thirty minutes and 399 runs, the highest at that time for any West Indian wicket against England and the best fourth wicket stand by any country against England. And that was no flash in the pan because he played in four of the Tests and averaged 64 runs throughout – the second highest for the West Indians for the series, well above Conrad Hunte, Kanhai, Clive Walcott, Solomon, and Butcher. At this stage, Frank had still not been recalled to the West Indian captaincy – in fact he was not the most popular figure in West Indian cricket. His greatest contribution to the game was still to come, culminating in highly successful tours as captain to Australia in 1960–61 (remember that famous tied Test in Brisbane?) and to England in 1963 when he and I were ranged against each other.

His rightful claim to fame at this time was that he combined the roles of captain and politician to weld together the interests and aspirations of West Indian cricketers from all the different islands. He was able also to control and satisfy the emergent feelings of all black cricket enthusiasts manifested in the growing practice of picking black players only.

But in the context of this book, it is for his batting, pure and simple, that we judge him. Even as he grew older, the elegance and artistry of his play remained whenever he had the opportunity to develop these skills for long enough. I say for long enough because at this stage in his career he was not safe early in his innings against good fast bowling – which applies to almost every batsman as he gets on in years, although it's sometimes fascinating to see older players, once they get attuned to the pace, however fast that may be, handle it just as well, if not better, than in their younger days.

His style was such that he might have been brought up in the English school rather than the predominantly harder-hitting and more back-foot style typical of West Indies. He was a side-on player, could play off both front and back foot, a good cutter square of the wicket, but less of a hooker than some of his compatriots. He was unquestionably at his best against slow bowling of all kinds, without using his feet to get to the pitch of the ball. He is therefore a rare exception to my general rule that the best players of spin bowling leave their crease and therefore dictate the length. Frank Worrell was an expert in sympathising with the spin and flight to make this unnecessary, and could score fluently and frequently as a result.

Another definitive study of Worrell is Ernest Eytle's *Frank Worrell*, with chapter commentaries by Worrell himself. Worrell's childhood and youth in Barbados, scrupulously recorded by Eytle, has no place in this piece but one should record that he left Barbados to live in Jamaica where 'the Jamaican selectors welcomed him with open arms'. They knew they had acquired someone very special.

Worrell played his first Test for West Indies against an MCC side, not at full strength and soon depleted by injuries. Indeed it was found necessary to summon Len Hutton from England to give authority and strength to the batting. He arrived late but managed to save the day; but of the four Tests two were drawn and the other two won by the West Indies. Throughout the tour MCC failed to win a single match. In the Tests, Worrell scored 294 runs for an average of 147. Worrell wrote modestly; 'There wasn't the same degree of science in the game in 1948 as there seems to be now. The field placing was comparatively unimaginative, and, save for the brilliance of Tang Choon or Everton Weekes, the fielding was moderate and the throwing much less accurate than it is today.'

In 1948 Worrell turned professional and joined Radcliffe in the Central Lancashire League. It was a very demanding style of cricket: 'One learnt to cope with the swerving ball, the turning ball, the cutter, the stopping ball.' In short he had his first taste of the notorious English conditions. But he mastered them in the end. In 1951, by the end of June he had scored 1,000 runs and finished the season with an average of 112.93. 'Perhaps the real value of this achievement can best be realised when it is understood that no side is allowed more than two-and-a-half hours batting.'

But he was still able to keep his hand in where the first-class game was concerned, and, between 1951 and 1963, captained West Indies against New Zealand, Australia, and England. He achieved the pinnacle of success, he was an international cricketer of the greatest renown. Some still say that his batting reached its peak with his 261 against England at Nottingham in 1950. But I seem to recall that he caused a great deal of trouble after that!

After 1963 in England, where his team was victorious due to excellent leadership, he was not seen in England again, but I met him later on a Cavaliers tour. By that time, already knighted for his service to West Indian cricket, he not only captained the side against us but was kind enough to house a group of us at his home, then in Kingston, Jamaica, near the university where he was working.

Looking back at his most untimely death from leukaemia, as a relatively young man, I suspect that even then he was already suffering – in fact he had the distinction of being fast asleep at the time when he should have been making a declaration, although he put that to rights by an adroit manipulation of his bowlers as and when the situation demanded.

He was a gentle, quietly spoken man with firmness of purpose. He was a beautifully built athlete, a fine looking man, and, of all players I've seen, a beautiful batsman in all sense of that phrase.

SIR FRANK MORTIMOR MAGLINNE WORRELL 1941–1964

Career Figures:	Innings 326	Runs 15,025	Average 54.24
Tests (51):	Innings 87	Runs 3,860	Average 49.48

LEGENDS

D. G. BRADMAN
G. A. HEADLEY
M. HIDE
J. B. HOBBS
B. A. RICHARDS
G. St A. SOBERS

Batsmen become legends in their own lifetime. There is no statutory waiting time before the masses accord the respect that is due, as is the misfortune of painters, writers and even politicians.

Anything less than a century was a 'failure' for Bradman at his peak and the whole world knew his fame. His remains the greatest name in Australian cricket, as W. G. Grace's is the best known in England.

George Headley held that position in West Indian cricket until it was challenged in pure cricketing terms by Sobers who therefore deserves to rank beside him.

Why should I place Barry Richards up there among the Gods? Perhaps it is to appease the fates that decreed he should be a refugee cricketer, denied the chance to join the legends as of right. He remains the best timer and striker of a cricket ball I ever saw so I see no reason to deny him his place.

Jack Hobbs can grace any niche one likes to give him. He is slightly out of context in this book, but I wanted to have my little say about him and it would have been inappropriate and downright disrespectful to put him in any other slot. As for Molly Hide, she remains the big name in women's cricket and the female sex deserves nothing but praise for such enthusiastic participation in a male dominated game.

D G BRADMAN

AUSTRALIA

'At the back of our home was an 800-gallon water tank set on a round brick stand. From the tank to the laundry door was a distance of about eight feet. The area underfoot was cemented and, with all the doors shut, this portion was enclosed on three sides and roofed over so that I could play there on wet days. Armed with a small cricket stump (which I used as a bat) I would throw a golf ball at this brick stand and try to hit the ball on the rebound. The golf ball came back at great speed and to hit it at all with the round stump was no easy task.'

This is Bradman recalling his boyhood in New South Wales, where, after school and at weekends, with no friends nearby, he was left to his own devices. The blend of infinite patience and concentration was already established. Then, at twelve, he played for his school: the wicket was a concrete slab covered with matting. His team made 156. Bradman's contribution was 115 not out. His first century, and a portent of things to come.

And did I ever see Bradman playing? Yes, I saw him on the cricket field, but fleetingly, when I was a very young man, although I came to know him later on of course. This is a guarded statement, because, when I last saw The Don, it was at the Centenary Test Match at Melbourne, and I was afforded the marvellous opportunity of sitting and talking to him for the best part of two hours as we watched the cricket from the Committee Seats of the Melbourne Cricket Club – and they are not easy to get into, I can assure you.

It was an ideal chance to get across some views that I held rather strongly about the way the game was going. Not long before, I had seen the Test series between England and West Indies, in England, absolutely dominated by fast bowling, and very aggressive bowling as well. If that was to be the entire future of Test cricket, then I felt something should be done. My first concern was that the lbw law had, after its further alteration, gone too much against the batsman, and that right arm fast bowler against right hand batsman was becoming a very difficult exercise indeed.

Well, The Don, having been a right hand batsman who had not had much trouble with bowlers of any sort, reacted rather aggressively to this suggestion, and it was not until we had argued the toss for a further quarter of an hour that I seemed to bridge the generation gap and, indeed, achieved a worthwhile conversation. Quickly apparent was the breadth of knowledge and vision for the future that was in Sir Donald Bradman's mind. His main point was that there had been much piecemeal meddling with the construction of the game and the laws, and that, when the next round of alterations came along, they should be comprehensive and not just further to what is already quite a mess.

He wasted little time in talking about how much polishing of the ball there should be by fielders or bowlers, or what restrictions there should be before considering all the other aspects, such as the actual style and manufacture of the ball, the type of pitch prepared which affects the wear on the ball, the types of fertiliser used on the outfield, how many times the outfield should be cut – and so forth. This very detailed analysis of the game indicates the sort of computer mind which can deal with a lot of information at one time and do so very quickly. This rare gift is probably what made The Don the batsman he was.

It has never been easy to 'know' this courteous but essentially taciturn man. Even when writing about himself in, say, *Farewell to Cricket* or *The Art of Batting*, there is (for all the technical finesse from the mind of a master, and the very correct and marked ability to cope with the awesome social chores of a Test captain) a feeling that, rather like a sharp chance in the slips, he has slipped through your fingers. Certainly I claim no special insight, but all those who played – and wrote about him in his prime – seem, to me, to have had great difficulty in getting his measure. Getting him out was the other problem. There may be a link between the two.

Perhaps the best study of this enigmatic man is by A. G. Moyes. He suggests that the young, emergent batting genius was soon to discover pockets of envy and enmity: 'The armour of reserve was forced on him, and he never lost it, because throughout his career there were always some, even among his team-mates, who seized every opportunity to hurt. All this helped to develop the character of the man, and it created a trace of dourness that was not natural.' Too much, too soon, perhaps. Now I do not wish to be 'compared' with Bradman or indeed any other batsman, but in the context of environment, upbringing and opportunity, Bradman and I may have one thing in common – 'the armour of reserve'. He seems to have had his thrust upon him. I have always thought that I was born with mine.

On Bradman the batsman, Moyes, surely, must be hard to beat. I quote him in full: 'Bradman used a grip all his own – "incorrect" others called it, because it was so unusual. Both hands were turned over the handle so that it

A cricketing legend at work. Bradman was particularly strong on the on side and no stroke typified his style of play more than the pull at which he was a master. His total concentration, and perfect balance at the end of the stroke, are well demonstrated in this photograph.

rested against the ball of the right thumb, while the fingers of the left hand were hidden from possible injury. It was this grip that made him the most venomous hooker in the game, for it turned the bat over the ball and kept it on the ground. No other first-class cricketer had this gift, which operated the same way with the cut, a stroke that he played magnificently. The only weakness in the novel grip was in cover-driving – this was only relative – and in meeting the ball that went away quickly from the bat. But his on-side play was a delight, and he could drive straight with power and certainty. Above all his concentration was amazing. He could be deaf to everything but the ticking of the clock if the game was to be saved, and he could move like a whirlwind when the time came for aggression . : . Bradman was not a stylist, but he had plenty of style and appealed strongly to the crowd. No other batsman in the history of cricket has been such an attracter of custom.'

The point was that Bradman had everything and I have been particularly surprised, when in speaking to his contemporaries, to find the extent to which they admired his aggression and his dynamism. Of course, what appealed to crowds immediately, was that he got on with it right from the start. He was an avid compiler of runs, a tremendous runner between wickets, and he never let the game stand still if he could possibly avoid it.

Now, I scarcely saw him play, and, when I did, he was an 'old' man and did not last very long. I saw him caught round the corner off Alec Bedser by Len Hutton. I have a feeling that he was dropped first and then caught later on. I saw him once again, when he came out of a long retirement at the request of Mr Menzies – a very short story reserved for the end of this piece.

So my comments on his style are based on hearsay, pictures, books, and everything that has been written about him; but, like all the really great batsmen, he based his play on a damaging attention to anything that the bowlers dropped short. Legend has it that his best stroke was the pull, flat bat, through mid wicket. This seems to be borne out by the way Bradman still talks about what batting can be and what it should be.

But it goes without saying, and you only have to look at his book, *The Art of Cricket*, to know that what people talk of as 'an unorthodox style' was really nothing of the sort. Possibly the grip is a little stronger in the right hand, the left hand a little more behind the bat handle than purists might advocate, but everything else is so much in the right place – the swing of the bat, the end of the bat pointing upwards, well above his hands, a lovely shoulder position, immaculate footwork, everything in the right place at the right time. Of course, if that kind of thing comes naturally, which it probably did to The Don, so much the better, like the very best golfers who don't have to think about the way they are doing it, they do it right from the word go.

Bradman's rise to fame began in 1927 when he was nineteen. Playing for New South Wales against South Australia, he scored 118 and 33. The next year in his first game against an England touring side, he scored 87 and 132, throwing out Wally Hammond into the bargain. In the first Test, on a rain-affected wicket, he made 18 and 1. In the second Test he was twelfth man; in the third he made 79 and 112, in the fourth, 40 and 58. At the end of his first Test series he had scored 466 for an average of 67.00. In 1929–30, playing for New South Wales against Queensland, he hit 452 out of 739. And so to England in 1930 with an Australian side eager to recover the Ashes: in his first game in England he scored, against Worcester, 236 in 268 minutes. In the first Test, he made 8 and 131, in the second (at Lord's) he made 254, in the third, 334 (309 of which he made on the first day), and at The Oval, 232. His Test total was 974 at an average of 139.14. Neville Cardus wrote: 'If Bradman develops his skill further he will in the end find himself considered not so much a master batsman as a phenomenon of the game.' And so it turned out.

It is not my intention to plod through statistics – though Bradman might be considered a special case. Suffice it to say that in the following years he thrashed the bowling of the West Indians and the South Africans. It took Jardine's side of 1932–33 to check him. Harold Larwood and Bill Voce caused a lot of trouble and indignation in this notorious Bodyline series and Australia lost four of the five Test matches.

Talking of Harold Larwood, The Don took time off to show me, and a small group of other English players, some film taken of that bodyline series, shown at his home on an old hand-wound projector. We pulled his leg a bit about some of the apparently quaint antics of the players, but it quickly transpired that he wanted to show us that Harold Larwood, who had given him the most problems, was probably – anyway according to that film – an occasional chucker of the ball.

This notorious subject had been a particular worry in the previous MCC tour to Australia, during 1958–59, when so many of the Australian bowlers appeared to be throwing – especially the left-hander, Meckiff. Whether, in fact, they were or they weren't, they certainly proved too much for the English batsmen. So there was even more point to The Don showing us a film which (either that or something very similar) was shown subsequently by the BBC in their pull-together of *A Hundred Years of Test Cricket* at the time of the Centenary Test. Again it was apparent that Harold Larwood's action was, at times, slightly doubtful according to the modern interpretation of what is a bowl and what is a throw.

As I say, we ribbed The Don a little bit because also in the film was the unusual sight of him stepping back to leg before the ball was bowled, which is rare, to say the least, except in some tail-end batsmen, or those batsmen who are frightened of what is going to happen – and I'm sure Bradman was never one of those. But he took it in good part, and explained that with the bodyline system, with all the fielders on the leg side, the only way to get runs, when the ball was bowled at the body, was to step away and have room to play the ball on the off-side.

In his second tour of England, Bradman was said to be a sick man. Sick he may have been, but he scored 304 at Leeds and 244 at The Oval. He was appointed captain of Australia at the age of 28, and won the rubber against England in Australia. England in 1938 was another story. At The Oval he sprained an ankle and did not bat at all. But the young Yorkshireman Len Hutton did, and the series is remembered mainly for his painstaking 364. After the war came the mauling of Wally Hammond's touring side in 1946–47; then to England in 1948 with what many consider to be the greatest Australian side ever. They were unbeaten but the great man was bowled by Eric Hollies for a duck, after a standing ovation on his way to the crease where, to rub it in, Yardley's side gave him a rousing three cheers. That seemed to do the trick. He was out second ball in his last Test Match. What a way to go.

Back to the old enigma. What made the greatest batsman of our century tick? That superb cricketing journalist Jack Fingleton thought that he had the answer. He wrote: 'It was confidence that went a long way towards making Bradman what he was. He had, of course, all the other essentials of batsmanship – eyesight, gift of timing, splendid footwork, superb judgement – but these could not have turned to the great wealth they were had he not possessed the confidence to give them full play. Confidence oozed out of Bradman.' Well, there's another piece of the jigsaw but I doubt if the puzzle will ever be completed.

Perhaps (almost) the last word should be some delicate touches from Bradman himself. He wrote: 'Opinions are vehemently and dogmatically expressed by lovers of the game who themselves are entirely without playing skill . . . This fascinating attraction which cricket has for incompetent players is something of an enigma. These same people are able on many occasions to discourse most intelligently on the finer points.' He added: 'Maybe the difference between the mediocre and the great player is that the latter has either developed the knowledge of how to avoid errors or has an inborn intuition. Most certainly it is not luck.'

Actually I have reserved the last word for myself. It is an incident that occurred when I was captain of England in our tour of Australia in 1962–63. I quote from my book *Ted Dexter Declares*: 'Before the Fifth and final Test at Sydney we played the Prime Minister's XI at Canberra – captain, Sir Donald Bradman. We had gathered he had been having the odd, secret net to get himself into shape. He had not played a serious innings for fourteen years but, once the blood started to flow, he might well show us some glimpses of the master in his prime. He took a straight four off Graveney, then Statham bowled him a nice length, just outside his off stump. The Don covered up and in some perverse way the ball trickled from the inside edge on to his pads and on to the wicket, and the bail fell off. Shades of Hollies all those years ago.

I am bound to insert a brief flourish of those old statistics, but what a sight they are.

SIR DONALD GEORGE BRADMAN 1927–1949

Career Figures:	Innings	338	Runs	28,067	Average	95.14
Tests (52):	Innings	80	Runs	6,996	Average	99.94

G A HEADLEY

WEST INDIES

The Oxford Companion to Sports and Games is both good and thrifty on George Headley: 'He was indisputably the finest West Indian batsman before the Second World War, usually going in at number three in poor batting sides. Eight of his ten Test centuries were against England, with 270 not out the highest; he scored a century in each innings of a match on two occasions.' But further examination is required.

You have to place Headley amongst the masters of the game simply by looking at his Test average of over 60.00. This is the statistical divide which separates the masters from the fellow travellers. Around the 50 mark is always passable, below 40 means that there is a fatal flaw somewhere, whereas the number of batsmen who average over 60.00 in Tests can be numbered on the fingers alone.

The point that he usually played in poor batting sides with everything resting on him, which suggested that he might have made even more in different circumstances, might not be as valid as it sounds. After all if there is only one great player in the side, it is only natural for the bowlers to set their sights on the man at the other end. I remember our bowlers in West Indies 1959–1960, pursuing just such a course against Gary Sobers in his prime, literally bowling him any ball that would yield him a single and keep him out of harm's way at the non-striker's end. Sobers had a massively impressive run total and average at the end of the season but it has to be said that for much of the time the bowlers were not even trying to get him out. Obviously such practice is a huge tribute to the skill of the player involved, but it certainly detracts from the theory that the great batsman in a poor batting side is vastly at a disadvantage.

Headley casts a strange shadow on the game, which is possibly to do with his colour and the period in which he played the game. Writing in *Just My Story*, Len Hutton says: 'Both his style and his application were products of his youthful days in the sunny West Indies . . . He was one of the few great players of my acquaintance who was not good at driving off his front foot. Indeed he scored nearly all his runs by the square cuts, pull, and deflections, of which he was such a master. He had an open-chested, two-eyed – or rather, two-shouldered stance, and anything short of a length he "murdered". His wonderful eye for the ball allowed him to play it extremely late, almost at the moment when the bowler was about to appeal for leg-before. At that split-second, Headley's bat would descend on the ball like a flash . . . But in spite of apparent deficiencies in front of the wicket, Headley could play well in any conditions, a skill he must have developed through playing in Lancashire League cricket.' Good old Lancashire League! You toll like a bell (a bit cracked sometimes) throughout the careers of innumerable West Indian cricketers. But Hutton will not let Headley off too lightly and concludes: 'Yet, as cricket's most graceful shots are played to the well pitched-up ball, I always felt that, because of his disinclination to play off his front foot, Headley was never so attractive to watch as most of the other greats of my time.'

We can turn, yet again, to C. L. R. James in *The World of Cricket*: 'Between 1929 and 1939 Headley never failed in a series of Tests. In the interval between the wars only the computing Bradman surpasses his figures. And these are considerations which no mechanical calculations can adequately register. For almost the whole of his career Headley, going in first wicket down, knew that if he failed to score or merely to stay, it was problematical whether his side would reach 150.' But from all sources the story is much the same; a very great cricketer who (leaving aside the tributes to his temperament and fine character) went into decline where the first-class game was concerned.

Headley made his comeback when already into his forties. The story goes that the great man took the field amid tremendous cheering and clapping and excited speculation as to how the grand old man would deal with the new generation of pale-skinned cricketers from over the water. In is only on hearsay but I have a picture in my mind of Headley taking his time, twirling his bat, looking round the field, and generally making his presence felt, before taking guard and settling himself at the crease. Facing him was one of the paler palefaces in Surrey's Tony Lock, the famous left-arm spinner who up to this time had used his faster ball sparingly and with no significant effect. What Headley would have seen would have been a figure, whose sleeves might have been down or even flapping, making a rhythmic, but slightly shambling run, to the wicket. The crowd would have expected a formal defensive stroke to this ordinary everyday-looking left-arm trundler.

What they actually experienced, rather than saw because it was all over in a split second, was the stumps of their champion flying out of the ground while the great man was still in the most preliminary process of moving his

George Headley, whose Test record between the wars is only surpassed by that of Sir Donald Bradman, in action for the West Indies against Surrey at The Oval in 1939.

bat. What in the world had happened? Had he been ready to receive? Surely something was wrong and the umpire would call no ball, even if belatedly? It took time apparently for the truth to dawn that the great man's innings was cut short to the minimum by the fastest first ball of his life; it was probably the fastest ball ever bowled by Tony Lock as well! Another story handed down, which may or may not belong to the same incident, is Headley exclaiming, 'Man, this isn't cricket, this is war,' which would have been apt enough in the circumstances.

But one thing seems certain; in spite of Hutton's cautious asides, Headley certainly knew how to play the 'English' bowling. There I envy him a bit; I often had a little trouble playing it myself.

GEORGE ALPHONSO HEADLEY MBE 1927–1954

Career Figures:	Innings 164	Runs 9,921	Average 69.86
Tests (22):	Innings 40	Runs 2,190	Average 60.83

M HIDE

ENGLAND

It would be monstrously unfair if women's cricket were to be ignored in this book, though this remark alone will certainly be regarded with suspicion by some women, even if they're not cricketers. We are fortunate to have a modern study: *Fair Play: The Story of Women's Cricket* by two very eminent ladies, Rachael Heyhoe Flint and Netta Rheinberg.

I have the greatest regard for women in sport except where they attempt to vie with men strength for strength. Neither am I keen on women's sport where strength, and the development thereof, is the crucial factor between success and failure, even when the competitors are all women. At the same time, if women wish to take on men at games of skill or games of chance, I can only say good luck to them. The areas of such competition are immense and in many, women have proved themselves the equal, and even the superior, of the more muscular male. In particular women have gained great success in show-jumping and the other equestrian sports (including, to a lesser degree, race riding, both on the flat and over jumps). But it would be good to see more women competitors in darts, snooker, rifleshooting, and other sports and pastimes where strength takes second place to skill.

I have reservations about women's cricket because it is clearly an advantage to be able to hit the ball harder than another batsman, and it needs strength to bowl fast, and power to throw the ball full pitch from the boundary. The women's cricket I have seen suffers, therefore, from a certain basic lack of muscle, and is usually dominated by those who have at least their fair share of strength. They fall into a similar category to lady golfers who, although their tenacity and competitiveness compares with that of the men, are unable to flight and control the ball with anything like the same skill. They tend to seek for length above all else, usually playing courses too long for them, and the winner often turns out to be the long hitter who is putting well that day. As for Molly Hide, she seemed to be a strong woman,

M HIDE

Molly Hide was one of the greatest women cricketers of all time. She was in the first women's England touring party to Australia and remained at the very top of women's cricket for a considerable length of time.

of average build, who was probably enough of a stylist not to bother with this lust for power.

She spent a long time at the top. When the English women made their first tour of Australia (and, characteristically, paid for their own passages and equipment), 'Molly Hide, later to captain England from 1937–9 and 1945–54, already showed a brilliance which was to shine steadily thereafter . . .'

Molly Hide writes only too briefly about her involvement in the game. There is a nice social touch: 'During the third Test at Sydney in 1949, both teams were allowed to use the men's dressing room in the main pavilion . . . As we had to go to a farewell reception on the last day, our long evening dresses hung from hooks on the walls . . .' As for the cricket, the captain speaks: 'My main objectives were always to play bright and attractive cricket, and to try to get a definite result in any match . . . The main problem on any tour is to give all players as much match practice as possible, and, at the same time, give the probable Test team the opportunity together as a team against as strong an opposition as possible.' She adds: 'The team should get on well together . . . they should be good mixers . . . they should be able to look on the humorous side of any situation which may arise.'

MOLLY HIDE

Against Australia:	Innings	19	Runs	608	Average	38.00
Against New Zealand:	Innings	5	Runs	264	Average	33.00

J B HOBBS

ENGLAND

I feel more desperately inadequate in writing about Jack Hobbs than about any other of these great batsmen. I have so little first-hand evidence to go on and yet everything I have read and heard leads me to believe that, by not seeing Hobbs in his prime, I was deprived of a unique experience. Books apart, even second and third hand evidence is slender, but what there is shows him to be the complete man. At least I have no doubts about the extent to which he dazzled the cricketing world with his mastery and excellence when batting.

There are many hefty tributes: G. O. Allen: 'undoubtedly the greatest batsman I ever saw'; Percy Fender (captain of Surrey): 'Jack Hobbs was the greatest batsman the world has known'; and Billy Griffith, formerly secretary of MCC: 'Jack Hobbs was perhaps the greatest batsman of them all and certainly there has never been a man more lovable, charming and more humble'.

More immediate evidence is in the full length painting of him which hangs in the Pavilion at The Oval. If he really did stand in such an assured and relaxed way with feet, hands, shoulders, and head so perfectly placed and poised, then inevitably he must have sent a tremor of apprehension down the backs of bowlers. And there is a photograph showing him in a much more animated position, moving into the drive, where the left shoulder, which in the stance was slightly open to make for relaxation and an easy head position, has now moved purposefully into the line of the ball.

This change is so striking that it has convinced me that this is the ideal in batting, not just an individual preference. The shoulders should be open in the stance, and then the act of lifting the bat, if properly done, gives a slight rotation to the trunk, bringing the left shoulder into the line of the ball. I have watched batsmen experimenting with this approach and it seems to work every time. Anyway, it is a powerful antidote to the opposite approach which is so often seen: i.e. the batsman straining to stand with his shoulders

Two of England's legendary cricketers walk out to the crease. Jack Hobbs and Herbert Sutcliffe opened the batting for England in twenty-four Test matches between 1924 and 1930, seeing their side past the hundred mark on no less than fifteen occasions, a remarkable record.

fully sideways in the stance, which puts a fierce twist in the neck as the head turns to look at the bowler; then, the moment the ball leaves the bowler's hand, all these preliminaries are thrown to the winds as the left shoulder turns away from the line, with disastrous results.

Apart from the normal process of reading and assimilating, there is the odd clip of film I have seen of the great man, where he moves with complete assurance and accuracy. It may seem strange that this powerful sense of accomplishment comes across from so few visual images but they live in the mind nevertheless.

There is the further evidence of actually meeting the man and talking with him in old age, when there was a serenity and certainty in his feelings about life and cricket which was so impressive. I am not saying that you can judge the whole temperament and style of a man from the way he bats, but on reflection I think you can often make an educated guess. I've said in my introduction to this book that one of the fascinations of the game is that it reflects temperament so strongly. Nowhere is that borne out more than in the person of Sir Jack Hobbs, both as a man to meet and as a batsman to watch.

Hobbs was knighted in 1953 and died in 1963. *The Oxford Companion of Sports and Games* pays him tribute through statistics: 'Sir John Berry Hobbs, cricketer for England and Surrey. Known as "the Master", he was the world's leading batsman between the eras of Grace and Bradman, his career extending from 1905 to 1934 . . . Among his records are the highest score at Lord's (316 not out), the highest score for the Players v Gentleman (236 not out), and for England against Australia most centuries (12), and the record first-wicket partnership (323 with Rhodes).'

In *Cricket Prints* R. C. Robertson-Glasgow leads with Hobbs and doesn't waste time. 'Crusoe' knew what he was talking about because he had bowled to the man: 'Hobbs was the greatest English batsman that I've seen and tried to remove. He was the most perfectly equipped by art and temperament for any style of innings on any sort of wicket against any quality of opposition. He was thirty-seven years of age when I first had the pleasure of bowling to him. Misleading suggestions are sometimes heard that a cricketer, after the age of thirty, is tottering on the brink of decline. This is humbug . . . I have seen Hobbs described as a frail man. Actually he had strength of thigh and forearm far above the average, a strength which was concealed in the art of method and grace of movement. His footwork was, as nearly as is humanly possible, perfect . . . All his strokes, that is, all the strokes in the game, were equally strong and easy; they were of an even perfection . . . To crown it all, he had the gift of smiling quietly at failure and triumph alike.'

Then the dour A. G. Moyes had this to say: 'You might keep Hammond quiet – O'Reilly could do that – but you couldn't subdue Hobbs. He had the

Jack Hobbs hitting out in the third Test match against Australia in 1926, watched by a packed Headingley crowd.

strokes to meet any emergency, and on a bad wicket his artistry revealed itself. He could overcome an awkward situation because he knew what to do and had the capacity, and he was such a shrewd campaigner that he could trick the bowlers into playing his game for him . . . He was both ancient and modern – ancient in forward play, modern in defensive excellence . . . As a fieldsman Hobbs ranks with the great cover-points. He was quick to move because he always anticipated the stroke, and thus gained a valuable yard or two, and when he fielded the ball was in position to throw.'

Perhaps the batting and the fielding – in the first rank – are not far apart. We have the Grace Gates at Lord's and those erected to Hobbs at The Oval. 'He deserved them,' said C. B. Fry, not exactly an inspired remark – but I'm sure Fry's heart and judgement were in the right place.

There is a fine study of Hobbs as man and cricketer in Ralph Barker's *Ten Great Innings*. The scene is The Oval 1926, England v Australia, the last match was crucial as the previous ones were drawn. 'The post-war record read Australia 12, England 1, with two games drawn. The Ashes it seemed, had permanently emigrated . . . [In his first innings Hobbs, at 37, was bowled by a full toss from Mailey.] Andrews at silly point put everyone's feelings into words. "What a turn up for the book!" [In his second innings he made precisely 100 when he was bowled by Gregory.] "Hobbs", said Macartney, the greatest Australian batsman of the day, "played his best innings in any cricket. Even under conditions favourable to the bowlers, there are times when batsman play over them, and Hobbs' cricket that day overcame all the bowlers' wiles."'

One should add that Herbert Sutcliffe made 161. Barker continued, 'but it is inescapable that by the genius of his play and personality Hobbs steered the partnership through.' In that last innings, England scored 436 and regained the Ashes for the first time since the war. Barker makes an interesting period aside: 'The greatest batsman in the world walked from his home to a nearby tram-stop and took a three-halfpenny ticket to The Oval. This was before the days of the car habit, and in any case Hobbs, with four children to feed, and clothe and educate, could not afford a car.'

Naturally my own estimation of him was enormously enhanced by the fact that he was kind enough to say nice things about my batting! Vastly less disciplined than his own, it may nevertheless on occasions have brought back memories to him. At least I always attempted to play in the classical manner, and Hobbs was certainly among those I tried to emulate, however indifferently. Surely there is no greater compliment than to be picked out for favourable comment among the members of one's own generation by a master from the past.

It is hard to credit the stories and statistics which show that Hobbs made as many, if not more, runs after the age of forty than he did before. Would it be possible today, I wonder? The answer, probably, is that if you are as good as Jack Hobbs then almost anything is possible. It would be much more difficult with the predominance of one-day cricket, with all the related chasing around to be done. Obviously the preponderance of straightforward three-day county cricket matches, with no over limitations, gave a batsman the chance to settle, and play his own game which must have helped enormously in providing Hobbs with such a long and increasingly successful career. But born in modern times, I believe that he would have triumphed in one-day cricket and in all the other forms – doubtless to a ripe old age as well. Strange that I should eulogise this man so much with so few opportunities to gain experience of him at first-hand, but I feel that way and I make no apologies.

In his last days, Hobbs had a sports shop in Fleet Street. He mostly had lunch in a restaurant next door. He was the most approachable of men and his natural humility, charm and wisdom will never be forgotten. At a memorial service in 1964, it was standing room only at Southwark Cathedral.

SIR JOHN BERRY HOBBS 1905–1934

Career Figures:	Innings 1,315	Runs 61,237	Average 50.65
Tests (61):	Innings 102	Runs 5,410	Average 56.94

B A RICHARDS

SOUTH AFRICA

Richards, inevitably, is linked with his friend and contemporary, Procter, in matters of cricket in South Africa, the English counties, and the issue of apartheid. David Frith wrote in 1976: 'Like his contemporary fellow-Springboks, Barry Richards has had no opportunity to play Test cricket since the series against Australia in 1969–70. International cricket's loss has continued to be county cricket's gain. For eight seasons he has made effortless centuries in all the major competitions, forming of late probably the most exciting and effective opening partnership with West Indies Gordon Greenidge for Hampshire. Sometimes seemingly "undismissable", sometimes apparently bored by the mediocrity around him, Richards has for long exemplified the champion unstretched by the challenge of his peers.'

It must have been challenge enough for Barry Richards when I first saw him on the MCC tour to South Africa in 1964–65. He was still a gangly schoolboy but already showing the skills which he was to develop to no mean tune later on. In one innings he scored a scintillating 50, with an ever-increasing repertoire of strokes, until he chanced his arm once too often and was stumped when at least four to five yards down the pitch. The way he threw back his blond hair with a broad grin and a giggle at this miscalculation sticks in my mind. It could have been a forerunner of other occasions when getting out appeared to matter less to him than most.

Of course the attitude and reaction of getting out is absolutely part and parcel of batting. It certainly weighs more heavily with some than with others and it can only be a matter of temperament and experience. Perhaps it is the pessimist who, when getting out to a particularly attacking stroke, decides to delete it entirely from his repertoire, whereas the optimist may try the stroke more often and eventually come to perfect it – or at least find a compromise where it can be played without danger. Many batsmen have obviously achieved the ideal balance in this respect but it is a fact that the greatest players like Pollock, Sobers, and Hammond perhaps, were seen to

Barry Richards's aggressive approach to batting is plain for all to see. Undisputably one of the best of his generation, Test crowds have been robbed of a truly exhilarating batsman. Even in defence (page 79), the aggression is still there.

bat largely for batting's sake, managing to keep this uppermost in their mind. It is a similar equation to that of the artist with a choice between commercial work which will sell and the work that he believes himself capable of and considers worthwhile. Fortunately, the cricketer may expect to receive his rewards on earth rather than posthumously, as is often the case with the artist. Nevertheless, this apparently carefree attitude in the great player usually arouses comment and indeed criticism.

Michael Melford writes: 'At home and in England when he was well in, he has been wont to become almost arrogant in his contempt for the bowling and to take reckless risks . . . In Australia he went on, not perhaps with care – he scarcely had time to be careful when making 325 in a day in Perth – but without the same indifference to danger . . . But by the start of 1970, after making thousands of runs in England, he must have been just about the best player *never* to have played in a Test match.'

Richard's own book, *Barry Richards on Cricket: Attack to Win*, is, apart from its cumbersome title, a very detailed, technical affair, and is more of a coaching manual than an account of his life and times. Take chapter one, *Comfort at the Crease*: 'I always feel that the best batsmen are those with an upright stance. Try to avoid crouching at the crease . . . this will disturb the position of the head, especially the eyes . . . Keep your body upright and your head will remain straight and not upset your sense of perspective.' Very good. Succeeding chapters discuss defensive technique, attack off the front foot, attack off the back foot, building an innings, fielding and wicket keeping, equipment, captaincy, and the attitude to the game. It is certainly sound enough, but a bit on the dull side, we seem to have read it all before.

Poor Richards, he is a disappointed and deprived sportsman, undisputedly one of the best of his generation with hardly a tale to tell his children when the time comes. He was so good that even success could seem like failure where the contest was inadequate. The 1976 *Wisden* records a rather disappointing performance by Hampshire in the County Championship. 'Richards was again the most successful batsman, but he, as with others, had periods of inconsistency . . . nevertheless he scored seven centuries.' Well yes, that included scores of 159 and 108 in his two innings against Kent at Southampton. And in 34 innings he made 1,572 runs and headed his County's averages with 49.12. Not bad for an inconsistent player!

Richards played three innings for the World Series cricket side in Australia, including one of 101 not out, made 166 runs and finished with an average of 83.00. In the grand floodlit finale, in February 1969, he and Procter made a match-winning stand of 71, to wrest the game from some rather angry Australians. 'Richards', wrote Alan Lee, 'restraining himself in a fashion I have not often seen in him, played the incessant bouncers with faultless technique and placid temperament. "I can't remember the last time I batted for five hours" he said later. "It was a graft, a struggle and I had to keep talking to myself to keep going." Richards, unlucky enough to be born a South African and a genius batsman had waited a long time to play this sort of innings at Test standard.'

BARRY ANDERSON RICHARDS 1964–1978

Career Figures:	Innings 543	Runs 27,293	Average 55.70
Tests (4):	Innings 7	Runs 508	Average 72.57

B A RICHARDS

G St A SOBERS

WEST INDIES

Garfield Sobers, as all the cricketing world knows, is a very special case. His marks in class, judged by all and sundry, are amazingly high, on the verge of perfection. Take this from Sir Neville Cardus in the 1967 *Wisden*: 'the most renowned name of any cricketer since Bradman's high noon. He is, in fact, even more famous than Bradman ever was; for he is accomplished in every department of the game, and has exhibited his genius in all climes and conditions . . . he is a stylish, prolific batsman; two bowlers in one, fastish left-arm, seaming the new ball, and slow to medium back-of-the hand spinner with the old ball; a swift, accurate, slip fieldsman in the class of Hammond and Simpson, and generally an astute captain. Statistics about him speak volumes . . .'

If that is not enough, Cardus proceeds to analyse, most precisely, the age-old problem of comparisons: 'It is of course, vain to measure ability in one age with ability in another. Only providence, timeless and all-seeing is qualified to weigh in the balance the arts and personality of a Hammond and a Sobers. It is enough that the deeds of Sobers are appreciated in our time, as we have witnessed them. He has boxed the compass of the world of present-day cricket . . . And here we touch on his secret: power and relaxation and the gift of holding himself in reserve . . . The sure sign of mastery, of genius of any order, is absence of strain, natural freedom of rhythm . . . The greatest ever? – certainly the greatest all-rounder today, and for decades.'

Heady stuff, you might think, very much in the vein of all 'ecstatic' cricket writing when a master takes the field. But it holds up: Sobers was the greatest cricketer I have seen or played against.

I was also lucky to count him a personal friend, having played many times, both against him and with him – much preferring the latter, I may say, because he was formidable. He was actually the one quickish left-arm over the wicket bowler who probably had the best of the argument with me. By and large, I rather fancied myself against that type of bowling. But he also got me out with his other varying styles, out of the back of the hand with the Chinaman, the left-hander's googly. And without remembering exactly where, no doubt he probably caught me out, and ran me out, and did all the other things that he was most capable of doing.

He was one of those people to whom you could always talk about the game however much acrimony and bad temper there might have been flying about. I think he stood aside from the pettiness of the game most of the time and that was both his charm and his greatness.

It would be ridiculous to say that he would bat in exactly the same way whether his team had 200 on the board or whether they were struggling at 53 for five but there was something of the same repose, and there certainly wouldn't be any greater, grim concentration, furrowed brow or anything like that. He would get on with the business of batting, although he might not have played too many attacking strokes for a while. In fact, he was a master at judging the time and place for the right innings. The times he got West Indies out of a hole were legion. Of course, in his latter days he used to bat well down the order, not surprisingly, because he had already bowled countless overs. He had to be pretty magnificent physical specimen to get through some of those Test matches in the way that he did.

Later on as captain and in some of his very last games, when he was brought back to play for West Indies after appalling knee injuries and operations, he was operating like a man with no legs but was still immensely effective. He hadn't got the pace as a bowler any more but he could still move the ball, bowl a line, and give the batsman problems. When batting, he didn't really need to use his feet very much half the time because his eye was so sure and the quality of his actual stroke-making was so high that sometimes footwork almost seemed to be an unnecessary luxury.

There were, of course, ways of getting him out, in his role of batsman, but believe me, you had to think about it. And then – you never can tell – the plan may be sound, the ploy ingenious, but the (relatively) easy catch is put down, and the man who should have been out for 2, rumbles the manoeuvre and goes on to make 150.

One must tread carefully in these matters, but, in a way, Sobers was a promising young bowler and fieldsman who, without losing (indeed whilst enhancing) these skills became one of the world's leading batsmen. He ended up as the all-rounder supremo. That subtle writer, C. L. R. James writing in *The World Of Cricket*, combines a fact with the most delicate appreciation of character: 'It should not be forgotten that, promoted to open the innings for West Indies against Australia in 1955 when not yet nineteen, Sobers hit Miller and Lindwall for 43 in fifteen minutes. With all his varied experience, that spirit is never far from the surface; it can be seen in the very way he walks to the wicket.' Note those last words – they are the words which

Sobers was the greatest cricketer I have seen or played against. He was a true master with the bat. A natural stroke player, his batting demonstrated a fine balance between power and relaxation. A classic case here of the head leading the stroke.

count. It's a mastery, but the implication is style, presence, authority – or if you like, charisma.

Sobers had his critics. On the West Indies tour of Australia (1960–61) the fiery O'Reilly wrote that 'Sobers is classed as one of the greatest batsmen in the game. Yesterday, however, he forgot that a man with such a reputation is expected to adapt his programme to his team's benefit.' Not great prose, but I see what he means.

However, in the first Test at Brisbane, another Sobers emerges (and another journalist too). Phil Tressider wrote: 'The West Indies, with left-hander Garfield Sobers in a champion's role, today gave Australia's Test bowlers their most humiliating thrashing in decades . . . Sobers reduced the Australian bowlers to the effectiveness of a club eleven attack. It was a day-long orgy of blazing boundary hitting.'

Eventually, Sobers suffered the ordeal of captaincy, the last of which was that of Nottinghamshire where his game, inevitably perhaps, began to retreat into the shades. But one must not forget that occasion when, batting against Glamorgan, he hit the bowler Nash for six sixes in one over.

As one of the few who entirely mastered that 'small circle of concentration', he did so with the least outward show. When in the mood he was a holy terror and a delight to behold – as long as you were not bowling to him.

SIR GARFIELD ST AUBRUN SOBERS 1953–1974

Career Figures:	Innings 609	Runs 28,315	Average 54.87
Tests (93):	Innings 160	Runs 8,032	Average 57.78

MECHANICS

G. BOYCOTT
L. HUTTON
V. L MANJREKAR

I may have the wrong word here to categorise one particular method of batting. It certainly smacks of efficiency, accurate striking and long service, with only occasional breakdowns. To that extent Boycott, Hutton and Manjrekar are properly observed.

Of course they all had their runaway moments, when the governor was released, the revolutions increased and their normal cruising speed shot up alarmingly. But in the main they allowed the bowlers to set the exact pressure on the accelerator. 'Play each ball on its merits' is said to every young player, but there are few who can resist the temptation to preselect – to coverdrive the good length ball or to cut the half-volley. It requires patience and understanding and concentration of a high order to honestly react to each ball, on its own, in isolation, avoiding risk and letting the human computer come up with the right response, every time.

It is this kind of rigid control over their actions that has placed these men in a category of their own. Offer them some indifferent bowling and they would score as quickly as the hardest hitters in the game. But when faced by bowlers who knew their job, they felt that it was no time for playing around, for joking or pretending. Batting was like a slice of their life to these two Yorkshiremen and their Indian counterpart Manjrekar and it was more than their reputations were worth to treat a good ball lightly and get out – when the opportunity to hit a bad ball for four in the next minute might thus elude them.

G BOYCOTT

ENGLAND

I am almost bound to be less than fair, if not grossly unfair, to Boycott in the context of these thirty, and more, great batsmen spanning all of half a century. Man of the others I never saw and probably their reputations have been gilded when handed down from generation to generation. It is only human to remember the best and forget the worst, rather like mothers who have more than one child despite the worst pangs of childbirth.

But Boycott is too much a man of my time to forget easily his weaknesses, quirks of character, and those times when he has seemed less than a great batsman. I saw him play one of his first good county innings for Yorkshire against Sussex when, chasing runs, he failed only narrowly to win the game singlehanded through lack of support at the other end. I was with him on his first overseas tour to South Africa in 1964–65, and nursed him through a sticky period when he was virtually ostracised by the rest of the team for what they considered to be unforgivably selfish behaviour, both on and off the field. That he should subsequently run me out at a crucial point in the Test at Port Elizabeth, when displaying precisely those characteristics, is only to be expected by instructors who believe in developing a man's talent however awkward the individual. As one of the press corps during the last ten years or so I have had to write critically of him, and, as a television commentator, to make snap judgements. No doubt if I were to write this all over again in twenty years' time I would be more generous in my praise and could conveniently forget the less distinguished passages in what has been a stormy cricketing career. So before I forget the main purpose let me make a personal comment on his style of play.

Except for a brief period in Australia on the first of Brearley's two tours, he has had exemplary head, body and foot positioning, and remains one of the few moderns to stick purposefully to the old adage that cricket is a sideways game. His actual batwork has been less to my liking, with a slightly strong lower hand position, insufficient backlift, and a tendency to play low

England's anchor man for much of the last fifteen years, Geoffrey Boycott owes much of his success in the game to the exemplary positioning of his head, body and feet. The old adage of 'bat and pad together' is well demonstrated in this photograph.

on the forward stroke which has brought him a few unnecessary raps on the fingers. The other effect of this short pick-up has been to make him an upward hooker of the ball during those short periods when he decided to play in a more attacking style, and so to be hit around the left upper arm and side more than was comfortable until he settled for more evasive tactics.

That being said, there have been too few occasions when Boycott has been a dominant batting force and perhaps too many when he has been happy to play the anchor role. Furthermore, I can remember few long, flourishing partnerships accounting for his major innings. More often there have been wickets falling at intervals the other end while he soldiers on in a form of cricketing martyrdom, and I have always had, in the back of my mind, a thought that his continued presence has been a possible cause of the problems at the other end. As a runner between wickets he has also had problems, and there is hardly a major player who has not suffered at his hands once or twice while batting with him. (He has never really seemed to trust the call of the other player, and even now will always double-check the safety of a run by looking where the ball has gone rather than responding directly to his partner's call.)

However, it must also be recorded that on many occasions England would have been in a sorry plight without him. I believe I saw him at his best in Australia with Illingworth; there was also the tour to West Indies, under Cowdrey, when he was equally effective, and, by all accounts, impressive. I think his batting career could have taken a much more even course had he at that stage been content with the way he was going. Instead, he felt he was getting less than his due from the critics and set sail on a dangerous course involving new strokes, which were foreign to his nature, and demanding too much of his defensively-based technique.

It strikes me that Boycott's exploits and antics must surely have astonished the unswerving, firm-of-purpose Bradman, although in his playing days he had known some pretty difficult characters. It's that exasperating touch again: arousing frustration in his colleagues, in members of his county and committee, and often in the crowd, apart from those fanatical supporters to whom he is a symbol of excellence. All are to blame but Boycott.

In Wisden 1978, Terry Brindle of the *Yorkshire Post* writes: 'Boycott's character and performance are indivisible; more than any player he has been judged in terms of personality'; and again, on Boycott's return to Test cricket against Australia, when at Headingley, 'Boycott's hundredth century – in a Test match before his Yorkshire public – was indeed the stuff that dreams are made of . . . But the abiding significance of his hundredth century was not simply statistical . . . It was the realisation, vitally important to Boycott himself, that the public were prepared to accept his peace offering after a controversial absence from Test cricket.' But it must not be forgotten that the absence was entirely of his own choosing. He was picked for the 1974–75 tour of Australia, then withdrew at the last moment. A pity – he might have given Mike Denness a hand against Lillee and Thomson.

Brindle comments again: 'Yet Boycott the technician has rarely been doubted. He is compact, beautifully balanced, professionally expert, arguably the most adroit player of the ball off the wicket in the modern game . . . Boycott builds an innings, brick by brick, cementing each stroke to the next with that extraordinary power of concentration which frustrates good bowling and intimidates poor. His centuries are an act of will.'

I would agree that in Boycott's case it does seem difficult to separate the batsman from the man. But it's almost a platitude, a glimpse of the obvious; the same can be said of any cricketer, though few indeed have shown Boycott's skill at backing into the limelight. But having agreed to go with Mike Brearley's side to Australia, his batting, though of course 'dedicated', foundered almost completely, in 1978–79, under the multitude of personal difficulties including family bereavement, resentment over the loss of the Yorkshire captaincy, and a totally unexpected alteration to his batting style. (He became very open chested which severely restricted his foot movement forward.)

However, at the start of the 1979 English season, Boycott settled his differences with Yorkshire and announced, happily and graciously, that he would be glad to play under their captain, Jackie Hampshire. Good luck to both of them, and in the few cricketing years left to them may they shine and entertain in first-class cricket.

The prospect of such a happy ending was enormously enhanced, of course, by Boycott's vastly improved form in Australia in 1979–80. Brilliant play in the one-day Internationals, and a less spectacular but agreeable return to form in the Tests, made him the batsman of the tour for England. This is the position that he has always set himself to occupy and it is fitting that I should leave him so enthroned.

GEOFFREY BOYCOTT OBE 1962–

Career Figures:	Innings 782	Runs 37,624	Average 56.74
Tests (94):	Innings 165	Runs 7,115	Average 49.40

L HUTTON

ENGLAND

Hutton, like Bradman, is another classic introvert of the Thirties. He was very good at going in first and, frequently, staying in for a long time. He was wary, vulnerable, and quite brilliant, an old master at a very early age, and it is hard to think of him playing for a county other than Yorkshire. His cricket was as thrifty as his speech and his humour. 'What happened Len?' the journalists asked when, for instance, he had been clean bowled by Miller while pushing on from 70 to 71 runs. 'Was it that the ball came in to you, or was it leaving you?' Hutton replied, 'I missed it.' That's the stuff to give the troops. 'In an England cricket eleven, the flesh may be of the south, but the bone is of the north, and the backbone is Yorkshire.'

A. A. Thomson in his book *Hutton and Washbrook* writes: 'At fourteen the boy's skills were recognised. The Pudsey wiseacres, among the most knowledgeable of all cricket-watchers, admitted that he had every stroke in the book; all he needed was the power. His photographs at that time show him as a slim, slight youth, though he must have been deceptively wiry.' Just so, a hint of the Bradmans again. At that age, at Radley, I was a strapping young lad, well on the way to six foot. The culmination of my physique thrust me into a different style of batting.

But natural aptitude always needs the complement of a great teacher. Hutton had two: Edgar Oldroyd, 'a batsman of immense skill and resource, [who] on outrageously bad pitches, was reckoned without a peer'; and George Hirst, that great coach who inspired 'confidence in those who were nervous, making them play better than they knew'. The latter bowled to Hutton and the boy played him with assurance, and all this remarkable coach said at the end of the trial was: 'keep on with that.' That's how it should be done – precisely, no waffling, after the bowling, the terse verbal delivery. Worse was to follow, and by 'worse' I mean the burden of acclaim.

Enter Herbert Sutcliffe: 'Hutton has not yet received his Yorkshire cap, and he is no more than eighteen years old, but I am bold enough to say that he is a certainty for a place as England's opening batsman. He is a marvel, the discovery of a generation.' There is another tribute – with an affectionate sting in the tail – from Neville Cardus, who according to Thomson 'merits the title of the Great Cricket Writer just as clearly as W. G. Grace deserves the title of the Great Cricketer . . .' Cardus wrote: 'Hutton never seemed to be learning or advancing, he had learnt it all by the first time he played for Yorkshire, even though he got a duck . . .'

Around that time an eighteen-year-old, Cyril Washbrook, playing for Lancashire Second, made a double century, while Hutton pressed on with another duck. It's a hard game, both in boyhood and manhood. The 'ability' is no good without the guts and the will-power. If you're any good at all, you can, as you get older, cut a few corners in the art of batting, but it can be a long day's journey into night. Batting was obviously in Hutton's blood, captaincy less so. This step into new responsibilities and stress was not to be taken lightly.

In *Just My Story*, Hutton makes the point very plainly: 'Wally Hammond had given up his professional status before the war and had turned amateur before captaining England. I was determined never to take a similar step. When I was sounded on the subject on my return from Australia in 1951, my reply was: "If I am to captain England I will do so only as a professional."' So in 1952 Hutton became the first professional to captain England – against India. It was a dismal affair (especially for India). The following year the Australians were back (with Bradman in the press-box and Hassett as captain in the field). Miller and Lindwall were back again, too, but, in a wet summer, England regained the Ashes after twenty years. Hutton looked ahead to the winter tour of West Indies. The batsman was already in the shadow of the captain: 'My biggest search, as captain of England, was for a pair of fast opening bowlers, and the men I had most in mind were Brian Statham and Freddie Trueman.' Frank Tyson came later, and Alec Bedser was on the wane. Hutton's tribute to this great bowler is both acute and generous but the writing was on the wall: 'Although I recognised that his control of length and swing remained of the top quality, I thought on a true wicket he did not make the ball "hurry through" as of old.'

Then Hutton's strange blend of humour comes into play. It's all in the words, if you know how to read between the lines: 'the exacting climate of West Indies demands the selection of men physically able to stand up to the conditions . . . I admit that, at thirty-eight, I was not a young man but I managed to take a complete rest before the tour and I kept fit with golf.' Better still: 'the first mistake I made was to allow Freddie Trueman to bowl against George Headley. Twirling his bat, out strode George Headley, "King George" as he is known to his own folk.' But Headley was even older than Hutton – forty-five to be precise – and had not played against top-class

The 22-year-old Leonard Hutton is congratulated by the Australian team at The Oval, in 1938, after he had passed Wally Hammond's score of 336, then the highest score in Test cricket. He went on to score 364, which remained the record until Garfield Sobers made 365 not out against Pakistan for West Indies in 1958.

bowling for many years. As Hutton recalls, 'time is as relentless to a cricketer's eye and mental reaction as it is in waiting for no man.' And Headley took a short ball from Trueman, tried to hook, missed it, and took a severe blow on his arm. The crowd went wild.

This is where you need to know the man and understand the cricketer. Imagine him remembering this one ball, just one tiny incident in a lifetime of cricketing conflict. But it was a fast ball from a dashing young bowler which hit an ageing adversary, unable to get out of the way. Hutton almost feels the ball on his own body. Fast bowling was never far away from Hutton's thoughts.

Hutton was a shrewd business man – and quite rightly so. He never let the game run away with him, but he had a purist streak: 'Cricket has always been so much a part of my existence that it has occupied my thoughts to the exclusion of other things, particularly after I took over the captaincy of England.' Well, yes, it can be a nightmare. Take the two Mikes – Denness and Brearley – fine captains and devoted cricketers, but their Test Match batting suffered. Hutton hung on grimly to the end. He faced some tough and rough customers: Lindwall, Miller, Bill Johnston, Ian Johnston, King etc. In my time there was Wes Hall, Charlie Griffith, Lance Gibbs, Richie Benaud and Garfield Sobers. They could be very tiresome too.

I suppose the case against Hutton is best put by the astringent A. G. Moyes who, let's face it, had a slight bias against English batsmen. But he was always lucid and pertinent. Here he is on Hutton at The Oval in 1938: 'I saw Hutton accumulate those 364 runs in an innings that was neither thrilling nor boring . . . Hutton in those thirteen hours and some minutes of batting was a model of defensive morality; there was not even a minor sin to be charged against him . . . but the attacking part of his machinery had been dismantled and stored away, for it was not wanted on this occasion. Yet he was not dull, simply because he could play all the strokes so fluently. All that was lacking was the will to attack. If the will was there it was kept in subjection.'

During war service Hutton broke an arm which is said to 'have lessened his powers'. Who knows? Old habits die hard in spite of broken limbs. I cannot believe that this great batsman would have played a different game entirely. Personally speaking, I could keep my head down in a tight situation, but thirteen hours at the crease was never my idea of enjoying the good life of cricket. Hutton was patient and would prowl around with infinite skill, I was the tiger who had to break out.

In his writing Hutton tends to preach a bit but the true voice of feeling shows through: 'there are no trade secrets in cricket . . . To all young cricketers I say: "do not be discouraged by early failure – and if things go wrong, don't blame your coach. Look nearer home for the cause."'

On the great masters he is hard to beat. In the sixties he wrote, for *The Observer*, a brief obituary on Wally Hammond. There was just one sentence which lit up the sky at night: 'whenever I saw Hammond batting I felt sorry for the ball.' Also in the obituary, he wrote: 'Hammond had an extremely agile brain, which was the reason behind his amazing quickness into any position for any type of stroke. Time and again he defied the first principles of the game by making up his mind where to hit the ball before it had left the bowler's hand . . .'

Finally, consider this verdict on Hutton in that monumental book, *The World of Cricket*: 'Most controversial is his influence on the younger generation of batsmen. He was almost the first great player who habitually, at least after the war, played slow bowling from the crease, and he was himself for this reason relatively vulnerable to the off-spinner. A whole generation has copied him, and it is sad to think that so fine a batsman and so beautiful a stylist has been to some extent responsible for what seems to many one of the great weaknesses of modern cricket.' I know all about this because I remember one batsman after another in the Radley College nets pretending to be Hutton thrusting forward with a severely angled bat in an attempt to emulate the master, often with disastrous results.

I wonder really where we got hold of this image of Hutton in the days when there was no television and when, to my certain knowledge, I had only ever seen two days of first-class cricket and Hutton was not batting during either of them. Perhaps it was the fashion for photographers to freeze him in action always in this position. In any case I am sure we gained a totally false impression. I have since seen film of his then world record 364 which showed him often enough playing right back to the slow bowling, although that angled bat is still in evidence. Thank goodness I still had to come in the future comprehensive instruction in the art of playing back, from one of my key mentors, Cyril Coote, the Cambridge groundsman, general factotum, friend to University cricket over the decades, and gentleman personified.

Nevertheless, hero worship lasts a long time, or you could say dies hard. It was during my second summer at University that I first came face to face with the Hutton I had revered for so long at a distance. Given special leave of absence from exams by my tutors, I had already passed an exhilarating and well-played 50 in an invitation match at Old Trafford. The batsman at the other end got out and in walked the great Yorkshireman, already retired but still very much a recent legend.

He walked slowly down the pitch for a word with the young lad in the fancy cap. 'Well played, son. Keep it going, we need a few more from you yet.' Those words, or something like them were still ringing in my head and all positive thoughts about batsmanship had been supplanted as the bowler started the next over. I was soon out to a careless stroke but it was the least of my worries as I walked gaily back to the pavilion. My boyhood idol had spoken to me and my day was made.

Hutton was knighted in 1956. He made over a hundred centuries in first-class cricket and in one month, June 1949, scored 1,294 runs.

SIR LEONARD HUTTON 1934–1960

Career Figures:	Innings 814	Runs 40,140	Average 55.51
Tests (79):	Innings 138	Runs 6,971	Average 56.67

V L MANJREKAR

INDIA

I count Vijay Manjrekar as a key figure in my cricketing education. Until I saw him bat, at considerable length, when I led England in India on my first captaincy assignment, in 1960–61, I had never appreciated the extent to which a batsman could be in total – and I mean *total* – control of what he was doing, and of everything the bowler was trying to do to him. Obviously this can only happen on perfect pitches where everything is in the batsman's favour. But, bearing in mind that I had seen Sobers and Worrell in the West Indies only the winter before, this speaks volumes for Manjrekar's skill. It was the way Manjrekar could place the ball – yes, it was his placement which impressed me most, and particularly one stroke for which he could be remembered with reverence.

The stroke in question was normally played off the last or penultimate ball of the over, when he wanted to take a single and get himself up the other end. Now that may sound a petty claim to fame and not a very desirable one. But it must be remembered that Test cricket in India is a different kettle of fish from that in many other parts of the world. It moves along at a measured pace, very often in great heat, on pitches which give the bowlers little encouragement and therefore makes for defensive fields. Given this, you will see that dashing strokes to the boundary were not the order of the day, and that, in this game of patience and waiting for the occasional scoring opportunity, it was of some importance to keep the strike rather than to stand patiently at the other end waiting on your partner.

Manjrekar was a master of playing in these, his own conditions. That is not to say that he did not play well, effectively, daringly, and even splendidly, on many occasions outside India, and indeed he is well remembered for excellent performances in England. Nevertheless, it was his ability to place the ball unerringly off the straightest and best length ball bowled by any pace bowler to gain him a single towards the end of an over (with absolutely no danger to himself or to his partner) that I remember most.

He was amazingly adept at inclining the blade of the bat at precisely the right angle to run the ball away to cover's wrong hand or to allow the ball to come up to him and glide it down the leg side. Of course, placement like this involves not just the angle but also the pace. Hit it too hard and there is no single; hit it too soft and another fielder has time to cut the ball off; but hit it in the right place at the right speed and there is always a single, whoever the fielder is and wherever he is standing, and this was an art that Manjrekar had developed to a very high degree. The problem with run stealing at this level is, of course, occasional lack of cooperation from your partner.

I remember some classic encounters – rather than partnerships – between Manjrekar and the much loved Polly Umrigar when neither, as non-strikers, would be even hinting at backing up on the fifth and sixth balls of the over. Similarly, if they had the strike they would be pressing hard for the single which, if they were lucky, they might persuade their partner to take. Anyway, there it is – a lesson, if not learned, at least witnessed at some length and used to good personal advantage on occasions thereafter.

In his foreword to Rusi Modi's *Some Indian Cricketers*, Sir Donald Bradman does not give Manjrekar a mention. This does not mean that Bradman is short of perception and generosity. Like many great batsmen, Bradman's mind is apt to turn to the bowling rather than to the batting. 'Modi' writes Bradman, 'has interposed flashes of wisdom which players would do well to note and remember. One such comment was: "It is always better to overpitch the new ball, giving it plenty of air, rather than bowl short." Every new ball bowler should paste that truism on his cap.'

But then take Modi on Manjrekar: 'Manjrekar faced fast bowling better than most of his colleagues. He can look back with justifiable pride at the way he tackled Trueman and Hall at their most menacing. He was one of the few batsmen like myself who were better at playing the ball leaving the bat than the one coming in. He was an artist, seeking and achieving technical perfection.'

Modi is very shrewd. His brief preface is, in some ways, much more pertinent and incisive than Bradman's foreword: 'In cricket, there is no second chance. A single mistake, and the batsman must retire to the pavilion. A tennis player, no matter how badly he is playing, has always a chance to redeem a double fault or a rash stroke.' Precisely. Cricket is a game of isolated incidents.

Modi writing on Manjrekar again: 'He was a truly great cricketer. It would be hard to leave him out of any Indian side . . . but he was an artist of variable moods . . . He was greater than the statistics would seem to suggest . . . Like Vijay Merchant and Vijay Hazare, Vijay Manjrekar was cast in the classic mould . . . He had all the strokes in the game and, like a true master, appeared to have all the time in the world in which to play them . . . In the art of batsmanship he never seemed to need a lesson. If one quality had to be singled out, it was his concentration. He was puritanically correct.' Then the inevitable shadow falls; the age is creeping in: 'However, after 1960, his batting was confined to the business of keeping the ball out of his wicket. His main scoring strokes were a square-cut and push past mid-wicket. Yet he was a difficult batsman to dislodge.' This, surely, is an affectionate kiss of death to a man whose earlier batting 'was a thing of joy, not laden with ornament or flourish, but embellished with grace and artful ease.'

Like Worrell, Manjrekar was an export to the Central Lancashire League (1956–58). He played for Castleton Moor and in his first season scored 1,456 runs – average 161.77. A great professional cricketer, by any standards.

I marvel at players in the Manjrekar mould – among Englishmen you might think of John Edrich as a similar figure – who played their Test cricket extremely effectively but did it almost entirely through the offerings of the bat. Not for them the glamour of having the occasional bowl and taking a surprise wicket. Not for them the relaxation, the variety of performing great deeds in the field, haring round the boundary like Randall, or bringing off brilliant catches. For Manjrekar, fielding was merely a necessary part of the game, one to be lived through without attempting to gain acclaim or to do more than was strictly and professionally necessary. I remember neither his speed over the ground, nor his sureness of handling, or how he threw the ball, and yet he must have done all those things in my presence. It was obviously something he did surreptitiously. On the other hand, to see him bat for any length of time was to remember him once and for all, for his straightness and correctness, lack of fuss and above all for that knack of stealing a vital single to get the bowling as and when he wished.

VIJAY LAXMAN MANJREKAR 1949–1973

Career Figures:	Innings 295	Runs 12,832	Average 49.92
Tests (55):	Innings 92	Runs 3,208	Average 39.12

STONEWALLERS

W. M. LAWRY
H. MOHAMMAD

There must be a stubborn streak in any batsman if he is to reach the top of his profession. In some, that stubbornness can be amplified in certain circumstances to something approaching sheer cussedness. So it is with the Stonewaller.

There is so much to like in private about the quietly-spoken Lawry from Australia and the immaculate inscrutable Hanif from Pakistan. But there were times, as they batted, when it seemed that all life had left them. The bat would come down in the way of the ball as regular as clockwork, but all efforts to hit it away for runs were subject to the overriding consideration which was not to get out – at any cost.

The cost might be the slow strangulation of the efforts of his partner at the other end. A whole game, which appeared to be on the boil, could be cooled down to a low simmer and when these men had this mood upon them, there was honestly not much that man or beast could do about it.

It must be said that batting for hours at a time to support and finally save an apparently lost cause is as fine a way to do battle for your country as any other. Both Lawry and Hanif have such battle honours which are well deserved and nothing should be taken away from them on this score.

It was the in-between times that made them famous. The indeterminate periods when most people felt that they could have done better themselves with a broom handle. Then the slow handclap would start, the raucous shout of 'Give it a go, you mug!' (in broad Australian) would echo round the ground and the activity would proceed at an ever decreasing snail's pace.

No true stonewaller ever acknowledged a restless crowd, or a frustrated bowler or an opposing captain driven to bowling donkey drops to make sure the batsman is still physically capable of normal functions.

Total concentration on the business of batting to the end of play is too consuming to allow any byplay. The stonewaller bats on and on, indifferent to everything and everyone outside his private, restricted world, where the only freedom is time spent in the middle with clever opponents unable to gain a millimetre of their objective.

W M LAWRY

AUSTRALIA

In Bill Lawry's good-natured book *Run-Digger* (edited by Phil Tessider) there is a perceptive foreword by Sir Robert Menzies who was very fond of his cricket – and not a bad judge. He wrote: 'That he is the most reliable opening batsman in the world is, I think, quite clear. Of course, to the onlooker avid for sensation, he can occasionally be very dull and unimaginative. I have myself seen him in the doldrums, and prayed for a breeze. But I have also seen him in full cry, hooking the ball with gusto and reducing the bowler to a state of frustrated despair.' Menzies went on: 'A first-class cricket team which lacks good batting openers operates under a great handicap. The dashing stroke-maker who comes in number three or number four finds himself, if there has been an early collapse, a virtual opener facing the new ball. This restricts his style and may well impoverish his performance. But great openers avert this disaster and pave the way to success . . . I have seen many famous Australian batsman over many years. Such players as Ponsford, Woodfull, Arthur Morris, Barnes, and others come readily to the mind's eye. They were all men of courage and skill and concentration. But in the history of Australian cricket Bill Lawry will take an honoured place with them.'

Another man had his eye on Lawry. During the Australians' 1961 tour of England, Sir Leonard Hutton wrote (from the press box): 'Each time I see Lawry, the more convinced I become that he is going to be one of the biggest thorns in England's side for years.' Lawry made 130 in his Test debut at Lord's. 'Lawry, Lawry, Hallelujah', enthused Brian Chapman. Now this is a book about batting and batsmen and – to some extent – about defining their strengths and weaknesses, and trying to find ways of getting them out. When I went as captain of England to Australia in 1962–63 I had Lawry very much in mind. This is from my own book *Ted Dexter Declares*: 'Test cricket is a very tough business indeed and that "fight" which, Ian Johnson insists, "the public wants to see" might be better described as a bitter war of nerves and

W M LAWRY

As his Test average bears out, Bill Lawry was one of the most reliable opening batsmen to play for Australia. Rarely one to lash out, he provided the foundation of many a big innings for his country. This photograph is not particularly pretty, but the footwork is copy-book and the difficult hook-shot is made to look simple.

tactics, a war which both sides have been preparing for, a conflict where the temperaments and skills of the opposition is a subject for close study in the rival camps. You sit down and consider the opening batsmen. How are you going to get them out? If they stay in, how can you stop them scoring runs and so dictating the course of events? Now Bill Lawry made runs in that first Test at Brisbane; it took him a fair time but there he was making runs, very hard to shift. Before the second Test he took another hundred off us for Victoria.'

There was a long-standing theory that Bill Lawry was weak on the off side, mainly because he scored most of his runs straight, and to the leg side. But what you learned, only when you bowled to him, was that the half volley, even wide of the off stump, was still met with the full face of the bat and hit back whence it came. There was no swashbuckling slash across the line, typical of so many left-handers. Even the straightest bowling was pushed back slightly to the leg side because, again, that was usually where it had been bowled from.

It was this determination to meet every ball with the full face of the bat which set Lawry above many of his contemporaries. I am not comparing him with Neil Harvey who is second only to Bradman as one of Australia's great run scorers, but it is relevant to note their contrasting styles; Harvey so free on the off side and less effective to leg, Lawry, the other way round.

There were two situations when Bill Lawry could really cut loose. Against slow bowling (I remember him hitting the unfortunate Pat Pocock out of Test cricket for some while by a deliberate assault on him at Old Trafford), and against a fast bowler overpitching one moment and then bowling short around the body the next. These Lawry could dispatch with consummate ease.

To return to the 1962–63 tour to Australia, again I quote from *Ted Dexter Declares*: 'How could we spike his guns? Suddenly I came up with the answer. There was one shot he never played – the cut – he did not cut at all. He kept the bat close to his body and it was almost impossible to pierce this tight defence. Also he had a trick of just stopping the ball on the off side, particularly from the right-handed bowler who was not following down that side of the wicket, and then he would take an easy single. I decided that if we kept Lawry pinned down, not scoring any runs, not only would he get frustrated but the other batsmen would suffer too. So I told my bowlers: "Bowl short just outside his off stump, the place where anyone else would be looking to cut the ball. We will have two, maybe three, slips, set gully back for the one, bring cover in close to stop the one to the off, and hope to make him powerless and miserable."

'Well that is what we did for the rest of the series and after the second Test we shut him up for good. This is to show what a technical business Test cricket is. Bill Lawry, no doubt, soon tumbled to our tactics but there was little he could do. It was certainly not "brighter cricket". The ball was not being struck, we were not even trying to bowl him out all the time. We slowed him down to a grinding tempo and, although he scored two fifties in that second Test, it took him hours and hours, and in fact contributed to our winning the match.'

As batsmen, Lawry and I were miles apart, but his verdict on me is typically generous and perceptive: 'Did Ted Dexter really care whether he made a score or not? I fancy he never did regard a cheap dismissal as a personal disaster as he might have a beaten favourite on which he had invested a sizeable sum. But we always knew that when "Lord Edward" strode out to the crease somebody had to do something in a hurry about getting his wicket else there would be mayhem. He went out with the sole intention of carrying the fight to the enemy which was his most profitable policy. His defence was the weakest link in his armour but he was so rarely on the defensive that it was hard for bowlers to exploit him.'

True, Lawry, that tall, left-handed batsman, had a tedious streak in his batting which bored many spectators stiff. But that's often the style of many openers who provide the foundation of a big innings for their side: they can win a lot of matches. The performance of Lawry's life must remain the six hours and ten minutes he spent at the crease against England at Lord's in 1961, scoring 130 out of 238 against the hostile bowling of Statham and Trueman on a fiery wicket. No wonder that Hutton gave him an approving nod – and so do I.

WILLIAM MORRIS LAWRY 1955–1971

Career Figures:	Innings 417	Runs 18,734	Average 50.90
Tests (67):	Innings 123	Runs 5,234	Average 47.15

H MOHAMMAD

PAKISTAN

In *The Cricketer Spring Annual* 1953, there is a record of Pakistan's tour of India. It starts like this: 'Pakistan's first match of the tour was a personal triumph for their seventeen-year-old opening batsman Hanif Mohammad, who scored a century in each innings.' Twelve matches (including Tests) were played on that tour and Hanif played in eleven of them. He scored 917 runs for an average of 66.50 and headed the batting averages. There was more to follow. 'The tiny little figure of Hanif Mohammad', writes Colin Cowdrey, 'has become a run-machine second only to Don Bradman . . . His rock-like defence has made him one of the hardest batsmen to bowl out in modern cricket, especially in his own country. Although he can play every stroke in the book and hit the ball very hard indeed, he prefers to cruise relentlessly on in a steady rhythm.'

For all his other attributes, the pity of it is that, rather like George Washington who is mainly remembered for his truthfulness, Hanif's name will probably live on largely through his 499 runs for Karachi against Bahawalpur. It is still the highest first-class cricket score, although it took infinitely less length of time than his other record breaking innings, 337, which he scored for Pakistan against West Indies in Barbados in 1957–58. Long stays at the wicket were his speciality so the longest must be recorded in detail to give him his due.

A crushing first Test defeat seemed inevitable when West Indies amassed 579 for 9 and then bowled Pakistan out in their first innings for 106. Three and a half days' play was still possible when Pakistan batted again. To save the game, therefore, it was virtually imperative for some batsmen to smash the world endurance record. Hanif scored 337, which fell 28 short of beating the Test record as it was then, held by Sir Leonard Hutton, of 364 at The Oval. But in the process, Hanif set a new record for the longest innings in first-class cricket, batting for sixteen hours and thirty-nine minutes, 999 minutes in all.

It is inevitable to talk of statistics when talking of Hanif Mohammad, and high scoring was very much the order of the day in the West Indies that season because Hutton's record did not survive that tour either. Garfield Sobers, then only twenty-one-years old, making his first Test century in the third Test at Kingston, hit 365 not out in ten hours eight minutes, three hours twelve minutes less than Hutton took in his innings against Australia at The Oval nearly twenty years previously.

You can't treat Hanif Mohammad in isolation; it is important to mention his place in his family tree. He was the middle of five sons, four of whom actually played Test cricket; only the second son, Raees, missed international selection and that was because of injury. Wazir, the eldest, played twenty Tests and there was Hanif, Mushtaq and Sadiq. Unfortunately one

Long stays at the wicket were the speciality of Hanif Mohammad. He had every stroke in the book and, once set into his customary steady rhythm, he was very hard to shift.

can't list the number of Test matches so far played by them as a family because, of course, Sadiq still gets a game for Pakistan and may ruin our careful statistics.

Hanif, of course, started incredibly young, playing in Test cricket when he was two months short of his eighteenth birthday but that pales against his younger brother Mushtaq's emergence as a Test player at the incredible age of fifteen years and one-hundred-and-twenty-four days. A major fascination for me is how these master players appear, as it were, from nowhere, in countries where there is no established ladder to climb from junior cricket to the pinnacles.

Hanif was born in India in the township of Junagadh, and he and his family then moved to Karachi at the time of Partition as founder inhabitants of Jinnah's new Muslim state. Like most great batsmen, he tells of a great deal of early training and practice. His formative cricket education took place when he batted on long evenings by electric light on the concrete terrace in front of his parents' house in Junagadh. Apparently, in practice, tennis balls were shaved of their fuzz on one side to produce swing in the air, and a cork ball was also used which according to Hanif 'came off that smooth concrete faster than any of your English fast bowlers can bowl at present.' That would have been said in the late sixties.

I would count as one of his greater triumphs the tour to England in 1967 when he captained the side. He had had a disappointing tour in 1962, when he failed to do himself justice, arriving handicapped by a knee injury and making a moderate impact on the Test series with scores of 47 and 31, 13 and 24, 9 and 4, 0 and 3, 46 and 0. In fact he failed to reach 50 in any innings and scored only 177 runs for an average of 17.70.

This wasn't up to the normal Hanif standard at all. So he came back five years later even though his knees were in no better shape. Of course, he had the spur of captaincy but in three Test matches he scored 228 runs with a highest innings of 187 for an average of 57. He made 187 not out, out of 354 in the first innings of the first Test. He went to the wicket with the score at 25 for 2 and saw that reduced to 99 for 6 but then found an able partner in Asif Iqbal and they put on 130 for the seventh wicket. A score of 187 not out, out of 354 in the first Test of a three-match series when you are captain – that was pretty good going especially with dodgy knees.

I also have an abiding memory – and, search as I can I can't find a record of it – of a match – it may have been in the Cavaliers' days – with Butch White bowling to Hanif at Lord's. I can envisage this lively pitch and Butch firing it down at little Hanif standing there, still with a bad knee. Everybody was expecting him just to block, duck, and weave – I think he had probably done so in the first innings. Yet on this occasion, the little man hooked and flicked the ball off his legs and cover drove, as though to say, 'you know I can play all these shots, you can't teach me anything about this batting game. Those times that I've hung about for ages and ages, they have only been to uphold the honour of Pakistan, or to uphold the honour of the Mohammad family. Don't try to come in here bowling fast at me, thinking that I don't know what the game is all about.' It was a magnificent display and I'm certain I'm not dreaming it. But I do find it impossible to pinpoint it in the pages of *Wisden*.

Hanif was a very dapper little man, always extremely elegant. He was remote and slightly inscrutable – he reminds me of the great Japanese golfer, Isao Aoki, and in both of them I can't help but admire their quietness, their determination, their principles.

As a stylist, like all of the very greatest players, he was predominantly a back foot player, very, very straight in defence, but he had all the strokes, the cuts and the pulls. At five feet six inches he was on the short side, of course, which made it all the more infuriating for the bowlers when Pakistan was on the wrong end of the stick and he was digging in. In fact you must give him great credit for the development of Pakistan cricket. He was a key figure in their progress towards true Test status and towards their Test players becoming recognised as some of the finest in the world. Without him I doubt that they could have reached that level so quickly because he gave them the backbone they needed.

Hanif played a lot of cricket between 1953 and 1965. It is clear that he was more at home and more difficult to shift in the warmer climates. But his overall application, tenacity, and sheer skill at the crease must give him a very high mark indeed. Above all, one must not forget how very good he was while still in his teens. His outstanding promise was at one time linked with that of Ian Craig, who failed in a sense to sustain the promise of his youth into maturity. Hanif played his role to the very end.

HANIF MOHAMMAD 1951–1975

Career Figures:	Innings 371	Runs 17,059	Average 52.32
Tests (55):	Innings 97	Runs 3,915	Average 43.98

STRONGMEN

P. J. P. BURGE
W. R. HAMMOND
P. B. H. MAY
C. MILBURN
N. C. O'NEILL
J. R. REID
I. V. A. RICHARDS
C. L. WALCOTT

These are the easiest to grade because exceptional power is the most readily discernible of all the elements in batting. The fielders will be the first to know. Broken fingers are part and parcel of the game against the likes of Milburn and Reid.

I have perhaps done Hammond, May and Viv Richards less than justice by including them in the one category. Of course they are supremos, virtually legends as well, but I wanted to make a point about May at least. He could certainly wallop a ball with the best and once his kind of class was 'in', then Hammond seemed to fit as well. Richards is in because I believe it to be his power, applied so quickly and decisively to the bowlers' offerings, more than his overall technique and psychology, that has taken him into the highest realms. He is built like a middle-weight boxer-cum-swimmer, with enormous torso development, so he fits the group by his sheer physique alone.

What thumpers the others were in their time! The hardest hits of all seem to have come from John Reid, perhaps the shortest of all in stature. Was he trying to prove something?

That is just speculation. It is like the argument about the fastest bowler of all time. Was it Tyson, or Thomson or Holding?

The answer is surely that there is precious little in it between them – and in any case the speed of the ball is only half the story. It is the same with hitting the ball hard. These men hit it hard regularly into the right places against the best bowling. They form a memorable group of names, without doubt.

P J P BURGE

AUSTRALIA

Peter Burge. Who's Peter Burge? Well, I'll tell you. Peter Burge is the man I would most like to have in any team batting number five or six when a cause was apparently lost, because he might just be the man to turn the match entirely on his own. There are not many players who fit this criterion – and not nearly as many as you would expect go in first and bat obdurately right through an innings. This obviously needs great technical skill, concentration, and a stubborn will to survive, but it takes a special level of resource and imagination to turn the tide single-handed as Peter Burge did more than once in his Test career.

The time I remember most vividly was at Headingley. I was the England captain and Peter Burge cost me a Test match. Such individuals live uncomfortably long in the memory. I can still recall the names and faces of fielders who put down the crucial catches; of umpires who seemed blind to the most obvious decision at the crucial point; of selection committee men who palpably came up with the wrong formula when a better alternative seemed obvious. Thus I can write about Peter Burge at Headingley with certainty and with feeling.

The Australian tour of England in 1964 was plagued with rain, and there were curious goings-on in some of the Tests. At Manchester, the Australian captain Simpson made a mammoth 311 runs, Barrington made 256, and I managed 174. As for Peter Burge, I had already dismissed him myself – lbw for 1 run at Nottingham – but the Leeds Test was a different story. After staying scoreless at the crease for twenty minutes he began to open up and scored 160. *Wisden* comments: 'Burge looks a fighter, he is a fighter . . . no one has tried to curb his attacking desires. He favours the hook and many a fast bowler has had cause to regret bowling short to him at times . . . his display was reminiscent of S. J. McCabe's 232 at Trent Bridge in 1938. Burge batted for five-and-a-quarter hours and hit 24 fours . . . Australia

Australia's Peter Burge in devastating action during his match-winning innings of 160 against England at Headingley in 1964. All Peter Parfitt and I could do was to take evasive action!

found in Burge the man to pull them out of trouble and, once they had lowered England's colours, they took good care not to throw away their hold on the Ashes.'

Captains are said to win the Ashes. Bowlers often think they win the Ashes. It is not often that a batsman can claim that honour as Burge is thoroughly entitled to do.

Burge's climb through the ranks was by no means hasty. At the age of twenty-one, he became a regular member of the Queensland side. His class was announced with an innings of 103 against New South Wales; the bowlers included Lindwall, Miller and Benaud. In 1954–55 he first played for Australia against England, and the first time he touched the ball he caught Len Hutton at leg-slip.

Once established, like all first-class cricketers he had some very bad patches indeed, and, in the following years, his Test place was always in doubt. But when he did play and found his touch, he was deadly, difficult to shift and went at a terrific pace. *Wisden* wrote: 'Burge always considers he bats better against England than anyone else because he feels it is more of a challenge.' *Wisden* again: 'In England in 1964 he assumed the mantle of Neil Harvey as Australia's leading batsman . . . He has a good defence, but is at his best attacking the bowling where, unlike most Australian batsmen, he prefers to play off the front foot.'

I would add to this entirely accurate observation that Burge's was quite a stilted movement, which tended to give him room to hit on the offside. We used to post a forward short leg and try to bowl in at the leg stump, when he first came in, with a fair chance of a 'nick-pad', but woe betide the unfortunate fielder (often me) if the bowler pitched slightly short because no one was quicker to latch on with a full-blooded, cross-batted forearm smash than the mighty Mr Burge.

He was a big hunk of muscle while he was playing, and the last time I saw him in Australia he had expanded symmetrically into the 20-stone class, but an illness had trimmed him of four or five stone again by the Centenary Test in 1980. He was a mild-mannered man with whom I shared an interest in and appreciation of the noble art of trotting and pacing, which is so much a part of the Australian heritage. I certainly much preferred a day out at the races with him compared to standing at short leg with a bowler who thought that such a big man couldn't hook!

PETER JOHN PARNELL BURGE 1952–1968

Career Figures:	Innings	354	Runs	14,648	Average	47.71
Tests (42):	Innings	68	Runs	2,290	Average	38.16

W R HAMMOND

ENGLAND

I am aware that the compass of this book, apart perhaps from a subjective choice or two, is mostly confined to the best and greatest batsmen of the last fifty or so years. None has lacked recognition; most have been showered with superlatives from those who have written thousands upon thousands of words about the game. It is difficult to avoid cliches and glimpses of the obvious; 'the best', 'the greatest', 'a genius at the crease', 'poetry in motion', and so forth. All played the same game – cricket – the trick is to detect both the similarities and the differences. And so we move to Wally Hammond.

There is an obituary of Hammond by E. W. Swanton in his book *Cricket From All Angles.* Most of the material comprises a selection from the several thousand pieces, long and short, reports, articles, and commentaries, that have appeared in *The Daily Telegraph* from 1946. Swanton writes: 'There has been nothing like the calm serenity of Hammond advancing to the crease, and surveying the field after taking guard. If he made a duck he did so like an emperor, but of course, ducks were not his speciality . . . The basis of his batting was the massive power of his driving, straight and to the off, but he used every stroke except the hook to fast bowling. O'Reilly aimed to peg him by attacking his legs, but this only curbed his speed of scoring. He averaged 51 against Australia . . . In Test cricket he never played better than in his first Australian tour under A. P. F. Chapman when he scored 905 with an average of 113. But the innings that will be specially remembered by English followers will be his masterful 240 against Australia at Lord's in 1938 . . . The only limitation concerns his captaincy. On changing status from professional to amateur in 1938, he became captain both of his county [Gloucestershire] and of England, but in Test cricket at any rate, the glamour that surrounded his own cricket found no reflection in his leadership . . . The failure of the 1946–1947 side in Australia, despite the warmest of post-war welcomes, and an abundance of surrounding goodwill, brought about his immediate retirement.' But Swanton concludes that Hammond was 'one of the greatest cricketers – perhaps one of the greatest half-dozen – who ever played for England.'

Hammond was not exactly a child prodigy but he was to reveal prodigious abilities. Apart from demonstrating outstanding gifts as bowler and fieldsman he had by 1927, at the age of twenty-four, already scored 2,969 runs in a season (including twelve centuries). Cardus as usual, made no mistakes in his judgement of a young player: 'The possibilities of this boy Hammond are beyond the scope of estimation. I tremble with delight at the very thought of the grandeur he will spread over the cricket fields when he has come to maturity. He is, in his own way, another Trumper in the making.' Note again, how Cardus, a 'lyrical' cricket reporter – though with a hard core of common sense – is reaching out for the superlatives.

I never saw the great man bat but I have seen a very short clip of film of him and his contemporaries, including Percy Chapman, the hard-hitting left hander, and a fascinating glimpse of Chubby Tate bowling, with that massive

Wally Hammond driving the ball through the off in the second Test between England and West Indies in 1933 at Manchester.

barrelled chest and the effortless rocking action which sent the ball winging on its way. In that particular bit of film, there was no doubt that, of all the batsmen on show, Hammond clearly showed himself to be modern, in the respect that everything was controlled, and neat, and extremely powerful, but no flourish for the sake of flourish. He had great economy of movement, despite the free swing of the bat, and altogether a very compact style, with the bat close to the front leg in the vertical position on the front foot, and was very swift in the cutting strokes – the square cut and the late cut.

It is interesting to note that he didn't employ the hook shot to fast bowlers, and it makes you wonder, in the more aggressive modern period, when any batsman who doesn't hook is subjected to a lot of short pitched bowling around the body, just how well Hammond would have coped with it. He is only one of a long line because you could say the same of Sir Leonard Hutton and Peter May, both of whom made huge scores without actually making the cross bat shot to leg off the rising ball from the fast bowler.

My guess is that any great player, if he had been pushed (because it was entirely necessary instead of taking the decision not to for safety's sake), would have decided that it was a valuable addition to his armoury and would have used it more.

When Hammond made his first tour of Australia in 1928–29, he was in the company of Hobbs, Sutcliffe, Leyland, Hendren and Chapman – daunting. Yet by the end, Hammond headed the tour batting with 1,553 runs at an average of 91.35. He charged on throughout the thirties, and dominated county cricket. Yet another superlative, this time from Sir Pelham Warner: 'His method of batting is a unique combination of eye, grace, majesty and power, and above all of correctness, the foundation of the art of batting.' And so it went on, leaving Len Hutton to write (with typical bluntness) in his *Observer* obituary: 'Whenever I saw Hammond batting I felt sorry for the ball.'

'Cometh the hour, cometh the man.' Well not always, but sometimes, and with devastating effect. I have enjoyed one or two such sublime moments myself, but nothing quite like Hammond's in that Lord's Test against Australia in 1938: from *The World of Cricket* comes not comment nor analysis, just a superb piece of narrative and observation.

'England in the first innings lost the wickets of Hutton, Edrich and Barnett for 31, all overwhelmed by the terrifyingly fast-rising bowling of McCormick. Hammond walked to the wicket in this moment of crisis with an impressive sureness of tread, his blue handkerchief just visible outside his right hip pocket. He destroyed the onslaughts of McCormick with regal authority. From the back foot he crashed ball after ball to the off-side boundary with a superbly timed propulsion of forearms and wrists. The strokes had so much power that the ball, having struck the rails, bounced nearly half-way back to the wicket. In six hours he scored 240, including 32 fours. As he came back to the pavilion the whole of the vast crowd at Lord's stood up for him.' By the way, this article is signed NC. It's that man Cardus again.

My only meeting with Hammond was on the tour to South Africa, under Mike Smith's captaincy in the winter of 1964–65, just after I had stood unsuccessfully in the election at Cardiff South-East against Mr James Callaghan. There was great excitement that Wally Hammond, a great legend to all of us, was actually going to come and meet us. I suppose it hadn't sunk in that he had emigrated to South Africa. He was a rather mysterious figure – nobody really knew what he did or just when he'd retired. The trouble was that, apart from the pleasantries of the day and the actual cricket which was played, there is not quite the same fulfilment from a meeting of this nature. Hammond had obviously been a very fine looking man and one could see that his athleticism was still with him.

He could not have been nicer or more straightforward. Certainly there were no signs of the withdrawn surliness with which he was occasionally accredited in the Press as captain of the first England team to tour Australia (1946) after the war, which had such disastrous results. I won't say that he could have been any man off the street, because he did have that certain air about him, and you could imagine him doing all those imperious things which people attribute to him. Certainly the records are there in the book to prove that he did them and that's enough for me!

WALTER REGINALD HAMMOND 1920–1951

Career Figures:	Innings 1,004	Runs 50,493	Average 56.10
Tests (85):	Innings 140	Runs 7,249	Average 58.45

P B H MAY

ENGLAND

Peter May has perhaps been more generously – and justly – celebrated than any other of England's post-war cricketers. From English cricketing writers, in particular, he has always attracted special affection and delight.

'When Peter May announced his retirement from first-class cricket in 1962, at the young age of thirty-two, it was hoped that he might one day play again. That he has never done so is the reason for an appreciation such as this having been delayed for so long.' This was John Woodcock, chief cricket correspondent of *The Times*, writing in *Wisden* 1971. Then Ralph Barker in *The World of Cricket*: 'One of the finest English batsmen in memory. Slightly unorthodox in his grip of the bat (according to the purists), he nevertheless was never anything but straight in defence, while his attacking strokes covered the area from slip to fine-leg. Especially was he strong on the on-side, and woe betide any bowler who chose to bowl at this particular angle for he would be dispatched through mid-on and mid-wicket with an ease that bespoke perfect timing and precision.'

May's first appearance against the Australians was in 1953 (playing for Surrey at The Oval) when Lindwall virtually destroyed him. But he recovered from this and made the Australians pay for it in following years. He was to captain England forty-one times in six years before his premature retirement.

As Woodcock later pointed out, he was lucky to learn his craft on fast and true pitches at Charterhouse and Fenners. I had the same good fortune at Radley and then, again, at Fenners. A good pitch is the one indispensable factor when learning the arts of the batting game – or bowling come to that. You can't learn to bat if you keep getting out all the time; and the best safeguard that is a sound, well-prepared strip with even bounce. As this is a book about batsmen and batting, I must insist on emphasising the point. At school, we were encouraged to go in, swing the bat and hit the ball. You can't do that on a bumpy or broken pitch. Mind you, all this was firmly rooted in classical principles; keep your head still, wait until the ball's in the air before moving, use your feet. As a schoolboy cricketer, the endless practice of batting and bowling, and catching and fielding, *apart* from playing in actual matches, seemed to me to be the most natural way of life that could possibly be imagined. At this point I must give my personal impression of Peter May.

I am bound to exaggerate and possibly lend undue importance to the skills of Peter May because he was England's leading batsman when I joined the senior ranks, and he was the first England captain I played under. Just as a new boy at a large school will see the headboy about twice as large as life, I saw Peter May in the same light.

There are, however, inescapable memories of his excellent and forthright skills with the bat (I have not put him in the heavyweight, hard-hitting class, but by golly, he could give the ball a tremendous thump.) And it should be remembered that, although a quietly-spoken man by nature, with no outward signs of aggression, there was no doubt about his murderous intentions when he went out to bat. Certainly I cannot help making comparisons when I think of England players, and very good ones at that, of the last ten years who seemed determined to make the heaviest weather of even the most moderate Test bowling. That was one thing which Peter May never tolerated as an attitude, nor did he ever fail to give a strong lead to other players. He made it his business to instil confidence into his players, and, if he half-suspected that the opposition was below par, it was a question of up and at 'em and devil take the hindmost. The possibilities of being dismissed for a low score, and therefore suffering from an odd form of shame, never entered his head, nor did he allow such negative thoughts to enter the heads of his other batsmen.

I remember a New Zealand team, with a number of hefty, raw-boned, medium-fast bowlers who all had skills of a sort, a certain amount of pace and the ability to move the ball off the seam, but May knew they were not Lindwalls or Millers, and proceeded to demonstrate the fact. By the time he had reached 20 or 30 the bat was starting to boom and the cover drives beginning to sail high, wide, and handsome, one bounce into the crowd over mid off, over the bowler's head, over mid on – there was just no stopping him. He made a hatful of hundreds against this same attack in one season. It was a masterly exhibition of mental and physical dominance from someone who knew what the highest standards were and cared for them.

Another brilliant innings was the one he played for Surrey on a rare 'come-back' appearance on a broken pitch at Guildford against Sussex. There was a direct comparison to be drawn with his successor in the middle order, Ken Barrington, who was reduced to fiddling and pottering about for overs and hours at a time by a steady, but nor particularly penetrative, Sussex attack. May would have none of this trifling and proceeded to rip the heart

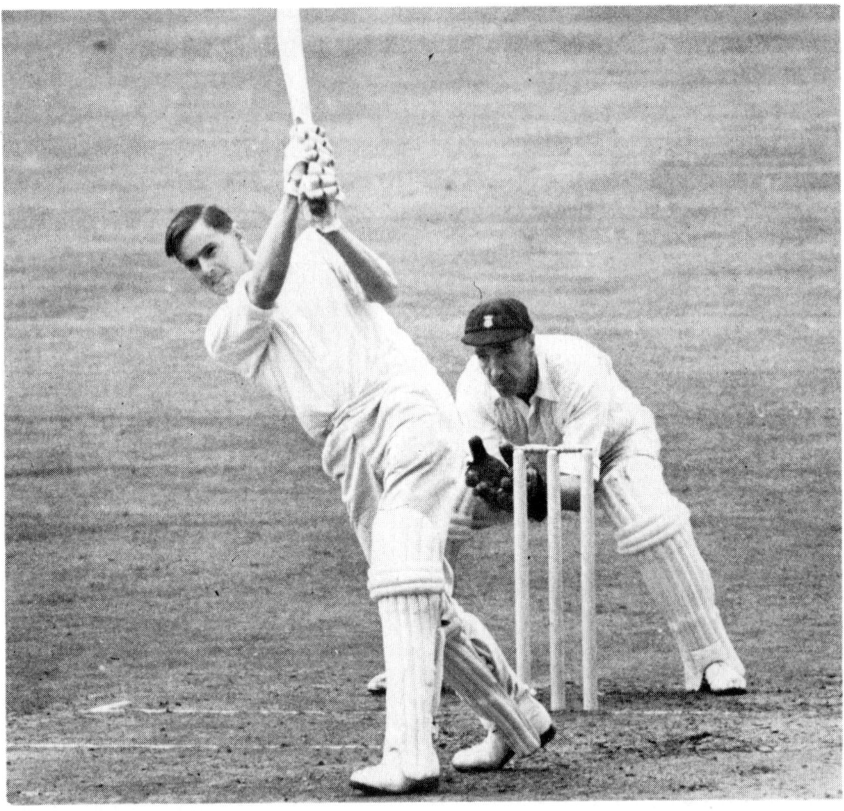

A classically elegant batsman, Peter May will be remembered particularly for his mastery of the on-drive, one of the most difficult shots in the book. His body position was always perfect and he would stroke the ball with tremendous power, making the shot look deceptively easy.

out of the bowling with shots off either foot, in the air or on the ground, both sides of the pitch, winning the match comfortably for his team and proving the only batsman on either side capable of handling the conditions in such splendid fashion.

Quite recently I sat in committee with him prior to the important seminar arranged for county coaches and the National Cricket Association in concert. May is not in the least embarrassed to repeat clearly the age-old outstanding basic principles of batting. 'What we are saying is that batting remains a sideways game. There are only two basic foot positions: either forward or back. When we play in defence we play straight with the full face of the bat pointing towards the bowler. When we are waiting to receive, we stand still, keep our head still and wait until the ball is on its way before moving.' These are principles which he employed with the greatest effect himself, and they can be recommended to anyone who wishes to follow in his footsteps. His only weakness, being tall and unable to keep the ball down on the leg side when playing off his body, was the absence of the hook shot against the fastest bowlers. This, however, was no great handicap and certainly did not stop him taking runs off the fastest and best when in his prime. By the time he went to West Indies in 1959–60, when the fastest bowling put him out of his stride, he was already a sick man with more on his mind than batting.

Internal bleeding gave rise to great concern for his health and immediate surgery was required on his hurried return to the UK in mid-tour. It is nice to know that the great man remains fit and well twenty years later as an active and effective administrator in the game which he served so conscientiously as a player.

Woodcock writes: 'by 1954–55 he was Hutton's vice-captain in Australia and New Zealand and when Len gave up the captaincy it was handed on to May. Still only twenty-six, he wasn't really ready for it . . . Yet here he was handling the England side at a younger age than anyone except A. P. F. Chapman . . . The last of his tours, to the West Indies in 1959–60, was also the least happy. He and his manager, Walter Robins, viewed the responsibilities of an MCC side in hopelessly differing ways. May thought they were there primarily to win, Robins primarily to entertain.'

Again, Woodcock is not long getting back to the same old theme of classic elegance. He recalls the stand with Cowdrey (411) for the fourth wicket (against West Indies at Edgbaston in 1957) 'which gave England a hold on the series and broke the spell that Ramadhin had cast upon England's batsmen since 1950.'

After failing to win back the Ashes in 1958–59, and then playing another season, he retired from the game to which he had brought such dedication, authority, and technical finesse.

PETER BARKER HOWARD MAY 1948–1963

Career Figures:	Innings	618	Runs	27,592	Average	51.00
Tests (66):	Innings	106	Runs	4,537	Average	46.77

C MILBURN

ENGLAND

The first time I took the batting of Colin Milburn at all seriously – up to that time he had the reputation of being a fat, jovial figure with a hefty thump in his bat – was on a memorable drive with John Arlott from a Test match in the north to the next day's county match, Hampshire v Sussex on the south coast. Arlott then was the proud owner of a nice R-type, or Mark 6 Bentley, and we took time off during the journey to indulge in an elegant picnic whilst sitting in the plush leather rear seating, using those delightfully engineered veneer fold-out tables so generously provided by Messrs Rolls-Royce.

Out of the blue came a typical probing Arlott question to me, then captain of England. 'Who', he asked, 'if there is a great batsman among the new generation, could he possibly *be*?' I think I named one or two possibles but without enthusiasm. My thoughts were usurped by that deep West Country drawl with the full burr and a throaty tone – '*Carlen Milburrrn*!' I though he might be joking but he went on to substantiate his comment and from curiosity as much as anything else, from that day on, I followed the fortunes of the Northamptonshire lad more closely.

There is a fine glimpse of Milburn by the ever-watchful Jim Swanton. It was 1967 at Eastbourne, the final day of Sussex v Northamptonshire. 'Parks's declaration setting Northampton to score 85 an hour for two hours and a quarter was made to seem all too generous, and Prideaux and Milburn actually reached their target with twenty minutes to spare . . . But Milburn! He began almost sedately, before, having got the measure of the wicket and the bowling, the fours simply flowed. It was one of those innings of which one might say one scarcely had to watch, only to listen. Wilfred Rhodes would have enjoyed it.

'Milburn played all the strokes, but his signature, so to speak, is the square hit on the on side, played with the utmost felicity of timing off either foot. Of his 24 fours (to say nothing of a six) most flowed in that direction. His hundred, in seventy-eight minutes, was much the fastest scored this season in the championship . . . Despite the speed of his scoring, he needed to take no extravagant risks. His weighty strokes fairly scorched the turf.'

A much later tribute from Ian Chappell is worth quoting. 'One man who could have reversed the negative trend which has plagued England for some years was Colin Milburn – a magnificient attacking batsman. England has had its share of shot-makers, batsmen like Dexter, Cowdrey and Graveney. Milburn perpetuates this approach of combining attack with sound defence. He was a carefree player who was prepared to chance his arm and his eye which meant occasionally that he was out in a disappointing fashion. But when a batsman like Milburn has his day, he can win a match.'

He could certainly hit a ball and I would rate him number one in that department when hitting square on the off side. Another of his glories, though, was the hook shot, played with devastating effect on a wet pitch at Lord's when the Australians had every reason to think they could dismiss England cheaply. His thundering hits into the top tiers of the Grandstand when Graham McKenzie pitched short still stand out in my memory.

The 1979 *Wisden* had this to say about his role in the match: 'Boycott and Milburn batted admirably after a shower at noon had enlivened the pitch. McKenzie was very awkward with his short-pitched bowling and Milburn, who made one glorious pull for 6, took several painful blows. It was on Friday that Milburn was seen at his very best. The pitch had recovered from the previous day's drenching. Milburn began his onslaught in the first over with a superb cover drive and a hook off McKenzie for 4 apiece.

'Cowper, who caused England so much trouble in the First Test, looked harmless enough under Milburn's treatment. His first ball was short and Milburn hooked it with tremendous power high and far into the Grandstand. The square cut, cover drive, and hook continued to flow until Milburn made his first mistake. He intended another mighty hit to leg only to present a catch to the ever-reliable Walters near the Tavern boundary. Altogether Milburn's memorable innings lasted two and a half hours and contained two 6s and twelve 4s, the last 68 runs coming in eighty-five minutes.'

Unfortunately I did not see another of his outstanding innings, a huge score, made in one day at Perth, which eye witnesses relate as the nearest thing to perpetual motion in heavyweight hitting and timing that they had ever seen. I must add a few comments about his eye injury, his occasional attempts at a comeback and why, unlike Pataudi, he failed to make the grade again. Both, in their entirely different styles of play were a great loss to the first-class game, but Pataudi managed things better.

Milburn of course lost the eye altogether – his left. Pataudi damaged the right but it remained with him, intact, and I suppose there must be a psychological advantage in that. Pataudi played Test cricket again and made hundreds, whereas Milburn's come back efforts were limited to county games with no great success, even though the familiar movements were still there and the occasional hint of the old power and timing. It is a subject in itself to define the percentage role played by actual eyesight in the batting process. Milburn and Pataudi have proved that much can be done with severe impairment. But then they were world-class players before the damage. It would be a difficult art to learn if everything were a blur from the beginning.

COLIN MILBURN 1960–1973

Career Figures:	Innings 435	Runs 13,262	Average 33.07
Tests (9):	Innings 16	Runs 654	Average 46.71

The loss of an eye in a car accident prevented Colin Milburn from making his rightful mark on Test cricket. He was a magnificent attacking batsman, particularly strong when playing square of the wicket, and in this instance the poor cricket ball has just received the full impact of a heavyweight short-arm jab!

N C O'NEILL

AUSTRALIA

The rise and fall of Norman O'Neill is well documented. He received more publicity from the media than any other cricketer of his time and could rank himself with popstars and politicians as to the number of front page pictures and column inches that he attracted. My interest in the man is more specialised, being a fascination and admiration for the cross-bat cut just behind square on the off side which he played with more authority, more power, and with more devastating effect than any other player I have seen before or since.

This was no mere stroking of the ball, or dabbing down, or glancing, or angling of the bat which do duty for genuine square cuts only because there is no ready vocabulary for commentators to differentiate between them. O'Neill's cut had as much in common with those insipid substitutes as a peashooter has with an elephant gun.

I admired the stroke while batting with the Cavaliers tour in South Africa, and have also taken the trouble to study it closely in slow motion on film. When watching it in live action, there was simply a blur of movement with a mighty flash of the bat as the ball was sent whistling on its way. The precise mechanics of the stroke could only really be evaluated on film. This revealed that his first movement was to go right across to the line of the ball with the raised bat in apparently perfect position for a straight bat defensive stroke. Then, as the ball rose off the turf, O'Neill would sway back from the waist to give himself room and crack the bat on the passing ball with all the power and precision of a circus ringmaster.

In other respects he was a typical player of the Australian school, working mainly from the back foot, and happy to drive the overpitched ball from that position, rather than move the weight forward again. He was powerful off his legs and an effective sweeper. Early in an innings a good away swing bowler could get him into trouble as he turned square on – Freddie Trueman

Norman O'Neill had the most devastating cross-bat cut behind square that I have ever seen. This was just one of the many strokes in his armoury which encouraged observers to herald him as the new Don Bradman; in the end, such a reputation was only partly fulfilled.

claimed his scalp in this way more than once. But once off the leash his hard-won confidence made him an ever-increasing threat to the fielding side.

However, let us go back to the strange story of this man whose star shone so brightly and faded so suddenly. In *The World of Cricket*, O'Neill is accorded an early tribute: 'Heralded as the new Don Bradman, Norman O'Neill became at the end of his first season, 1957–58, the third Australian cricketer to have scored 1,000 runs in the Sheffield Shield . . . His presence attracted enormous crowds and the sort of publicity which had surrounded Bradman a generation before . . .' I have been there before and can just manage a sardonic smile when it is observed: 'With such a fearful reputation to live up to, it is hardly surprising that he found the going hard at some point.' You can say that again.

N C O'NEILL

O'Neill, like the rest of us so-called first-class batsmen could be futile and useless, though seldom downright boring. But as always, the flint shows through in the end. Turn to Jack Fingleton in *Wisden* 1962. Fingleton, as all the world knows, writes brilliantly about the game, but he's pretty thrifty and seems to favour Australian, rather than English cricketers. However, he's very sound on Norman: 'After a short tour of South Africa before an Australian season started, O'Neill so impressed W. R. Hammond that the old English Test star dubbed him the best all-round batsman he had seen since the war. That was high praise. To be true, a high innings by O'Neill is a thing of masterful beauty. His stroking is delectable, immense in its power. But O'Neill has often got himself into a rut. He is a bad beginner. He seems to come to the middle as if he has been fretting in the dressing room, worrying about the future . . .'

Take Jim Swanton again with his *First Impressions*, and very sound, sensible and perceptive they have proved to be. It was October 1958, Perth. MCC (or England, if you like) had won three Test series running. There was a rumour that a batsman called O'Neill might fit the bill and restore the fortunes of Australia. Swanton wrote: 'There are the seeds of greatness in O'Neill . . . the physical equipment is obviously there. He is all but six feet tall, but the impression one has is of breadth rather than height. He is big in the thighs, thick across the shoulders, and wonderfully strong in the fore-arms and wrists . . . In the stance the blade is held shut, but the back-lift is pretty straight, especially for an Australian . . .'

Swanton goes on with further technical analysis, building the image of yet another 'great' batsman. But the wary Swanton leaves a footnote behind: 'Consistency of achievement, however, eluded him . . . His nerves were tightly strung, and when he retired at the early age of thirty it was with his high promise only partly fulfilled.' Through injury and indifference O'Neill's cricketing future was short. He slipped away into obscurity as quickly as he emerged.

NORMAN CLIFFORD O'NEILL 1955–1967

Career Figures:	Innings 306	Runs 13,859	Average 50.95
Tests (42):	Innings 69	Runs 2,779	Average 45.55

J R REID

NEW ZEALAND

I would put John Reid at the head of my heavy mob because, by all reports, in one particular season he hit the ball probably harder than anyone had done before or since. It is not difficult to believe because Mr Reid was not only a considerable athlete but built like a weightlifter into the bargain. Very thick set with massive hairy forearms, I put him in the Godfrey Evans category for an overall impression of sheer animal strength.

Of all my chosen batsmen, John Reid would be first choice to participate in the sporting television competition, *Superstars*. It is mainly to do with power/weight ratio, and although John Reid was no lightweight, I can imagine him doing armlifts on the bar and squat thrusts, with the best of them.

When it came to batting, Reid was no stylist although he was by no means awkward or unorthodox. Again he was a predominantly back foot player but given the right kind of ammunition he would release bat at ball with a 'batblade speed' (my cricketing definition serving the same purpose as 'club-head speed' in golf) which only the most finely engineered high speed camera shutter could freeze.

To propel the ball at tremendous velocity more than once in a blue moon also requires superb timing and body positioning. It follows that Reid's balance and movement of the ball must have been of the highest class. It was during the 1961–62 New Zealand tour to South Africa, captained by Reid, that reports came back of his awesome power. This was on the grapevine but it is worth quoting *Wisden* on Reid's contribution. 'The tour of twenty-four matches must go down in history as belonging almost exclusively to Reid. This quiet, unassuming master of bat and ball, smashed [note the word] most of the records open to him. In the five Test matches he scored more runs than any two of his colleagues. His tour aggregate of 1,915 runs eclipsed Compton's thirteen-year-old record. He topped the century seven times, including a glorious 203 on his favourite Newlands, and easily headed the fielding statistics with 22 catches . . . the bowlers never let up and Reid held pride of place with four wickets for 44 runs in a marathon spell of 45 overs when he won the all important Test match almost single-handed . . .' John Reid headed both batting and bowling averages in the Test matches, 546 runs at an average of 60.64, and eleven wickets at an average of 19.72. Not much doubt that the man could play cricket!

This hard-hitting information arose from my somewhat surprised enquiries as to how Reid came to perform so incredibly well, far above anything I had considered him capable of on the times I saw him play. At that time, New Zealand were usually having the worst of it against England, which can make cricket difficult even for the best players. In South Africa, Reid was at least leading a side capable of sharing the honours with the opposition but even so, it seemed to be a performance out of the ordinary.

The reports which came back gave the impression of a story for schoolboys: the man who hit the ball so hard that the fielders couldn't catch it! What a difference it would make to batting if there was no need to keep the ball along the ground. Just hit it at any territory and, as long as its muzzle velocity is high enough, and the fielders' hands are made of nothing harder than flesh and bone and sinew, then the batsman holds sway.

Was it really possible that John Reid developed the super power of an Incredible Hulk for just one tour? I can only relay the comments of the South African players who were ranged against him, and they swear blind that he did indeed cannon the ball so hard that it became a matter of self-preservation rather than actually trying to catch him out.

There have been plenty of other hard hitters in the game and I count myself as one. I must also include Colin Milburn's square cut, Clyde Walcott's straight drive off the long half volley on the back foot, and (although I have not written a separate section on this South African) Colin Bland's contemptuous hitting of slow bowlers for six. All these batsmen could certainly make the ball bounce back off the palings, but I doubt that anyone ever hit it harder than John Reid, particularly on his one triumphant tour to South Africa.

Reid started with Wellington in 1946, and entered Test cricket with two matches against England in 1949. W. A. Hadlee was the captain. Reid has been described as 'versatile'. 'In 1949 he was reserve wicket-keeper but he was also a more than useful bowler and a fine fielder . . . and he is one of the greatest batsmen New Zealand has produced. A powerful driver and a good hooker of the ball, he enjoys best of all attacking the bowler, but in his long career has usually found himself fighting to save lost causes.'

Arthur H. Carman wrote in 1946: 'New Zealand cricket will be remembered more for its style than for its successes of failures. We have become slaves to the stroke off the back foot . . .' Well that sounds all right. But you never can tell. Back foot? Front foot? It all depends on who is doing it.

In South Africa, in 1953–54, Reid became the first cricketer to make 1,000 runs and take 50 wickets in a South African season. He also had to beat that old curse of captaincy, against England in 1958 and in South Africa in 1961–62.

JOHN RICHARD REID OBE 1947–1965

Career Figures:	Innings 418	Runs 16,128	Average 41.35
Tests (58):	Innings 108	Runs 3,428	Average 33.28

One of the greatest batsmen that New Zealand has produced, John Reid impressed people with his awesome power. His timing and body positioning were superb; combine that with the speed with which he released bat at ball and one is given some idea of why fielders were quite happy to see the ball pass them by.

I V A RICHARDS

WEST INDIES

Sometimes someone with remarkable promise fails to reach full maturity and leaves a nagging disappointment behind, while others get better as they grow older but never set the haystacks on fire. Look back at many a *Wisden* and see what has happened to those selected for *Five Cricketers of the Year.* But where Vivian Richards (West Indies and Somerset) is concerned he has fulfilled every promise. As usual there is the comparison with Bradman, as we let Terry Cooper start to tell the tale. 'The modern generation of cricket followers were provided with an ample illustration of what the legendary Don Bradman's domination of the game must have been like in the 1930s by the exploits of Isaac Vivian Alexander Richards, the West Indian batsman, during the first eight months of 1976.'

The Christian names go on a bit, but then so does his cricket. 'In the eleven Tests he managed to cram into that period, Richards accumulated 1,710 runs with the style and consistency of a great batsman.'

I was forwarned of the progress Richards was making as a batsman in the April of that year when West Indies came to England after their Australian tour. They were having an early practice in the Lord's nets and their battery of fast bowlers were operating at a brisk enough pace on less than perfect pitches – brisk enough anyway to have all but one batsman shying away and taking good care to take evasive action. The one batsman who played without apparent concern was Vivian Richards, who seemed to have time to spare to hit every ball smack in the middle of the bat and to be minimally inconvenienced by the odd lifter. It was an impressive demonstration of batting skills but the question remained – could Richards maintain the heavy scoring formula which he had evolved during the latter part of that Australian tour (which had in fact started so disastrously for him)? Not everyone will remember that England's opening bowler at the beginning of that Test series in England was a medium pacer of no great renown, to wit Mike Selvey of Middlesex, and how many will remember now that Selvey hit

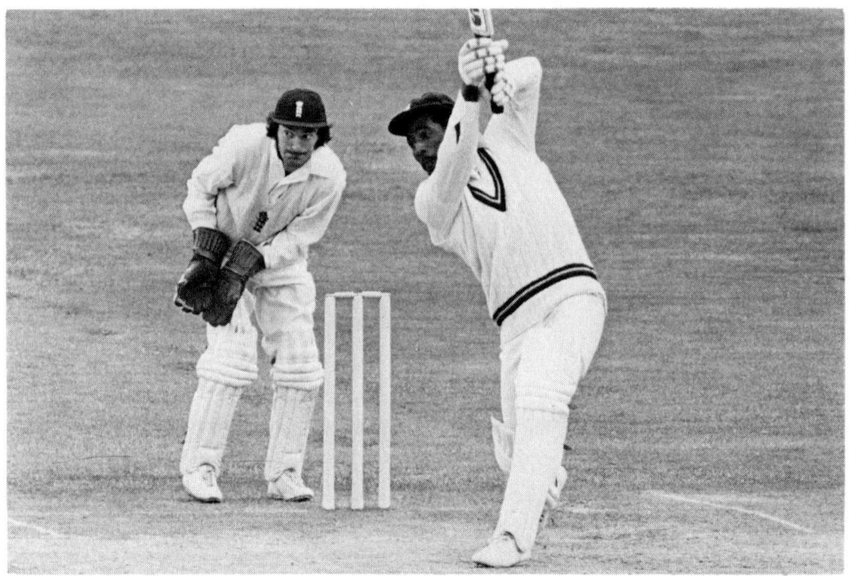

Undoubtedly the finest, and most exciting batsman in the world today, Viv Richards can drive on both sides of the wicket with equal ease and not necessarily off the 'right' ball for the stroke-hence making field-setting a nightmare.

Richard's middle stump with the great man's bat swinging wildly while the ball wasn't, with head thrown back like a man downing the last dregs of a pint?

After this indifferent beginning the record shows that in the sunshine against bowling of no outstanding merit, he helped himself to 829 runs in seven innings – including scores of 291, 232 and 135. His aggregate in the Test in England was the highest by any West Indian in a single series, and yet he was forced to miss the second Test through illness.

He was born in 1952 in Antigua, where these days every member of the island lays claim to have detected the promise of this outstanding player. We can brush that aside, but outstanding Vivian Richards certainly is. With help from the locals he came to England (accompanied by Andy Roberts) and to Alf Gover's cricket school. He went on to Somerset, and the West Indies Test side.

One can do no better than to turn to Tony Cozier with his ecstatic (but by no means ill-informed) description of Vivian Richards: 'His batting and magnificent fielding in any position carry the unmistakeable stamp of genius . . . From the earliest days he has hit the ball hard but always with style and timing.' But, Cozier goes on: 'Before Gover and Somerset and Test cricket, Richards would almost invariably do something foolish midway through an innings of great promise, and pay for it . . . his defence was virtually non-existent simply because he wanted to play every stroke that had ever been invented – and some that were not.'

What Cozier does not mention is the main basis of this tremendous repertoire, which is the uncanny ability to time the ball fluently on the leg side off anything remotely pitched up on any line somewhere near the stumps. For most mortals this apparent play across the line, or closing of the bat face at impact, would prove a permanent Achilles heel. When I watch Richards even now my heart is often in my mouth, thinking that he must miss a straight one sooner or later. The answer is that he doesn't miss, just as Denis Compton never missed his natural sweep shot, regardless of the length and direction of the ball, once he had chosen to play it. There is no accounting for this kind of genius and precious little that a bowler can do about it except to plug the leg side gaps as best he can.

I suppose Richards has given bowlers more of a headache in terms of where best to bowl to him than any other batsman of his generation. If I had a quality slow left arm bowler – and I mean *slow*, not medium slow – then I would be tempted to use him early on to Richards in case this turning of the bat to the leg side could be exploited. Even so it would be rather like backing a 50–1 winner when already thousands of pounds in debt. That is how the bowlers feel with the runs mounting up against them and with so little room for manoeuvre.

We gather that Brian Close at Somerset, and Clive Lloyd in Test matches, 'have taught him that only runs count in the book, not shots. With everything else, Vivian Richards possesses supreme self-confidence, almost arrogance – which I have noticed in few cricketers apart from Sobers – and an uninhibited enjoyment of the game. Like Sobers and almost all other great players he has taken his fame in his stride.'

There seems to be a slight contradiction here. But when in full flow, he is a joy to behold, that I would never deny. Like all great batsmen he pulls in the crowds and sends a ripple through them when he walks to the crease. But for balance here is Terry Cooper's final paragraph in his *Wisden* piece: 'Self-confidence, without arrogance is one of Richards' hallmarks . . . another is the unconfined enjoyment he gets out of the game. Both will be tested when he is forced to endure the barren periods which are the lot of all cricketers, great and humble alike . . .' They do go on a bit these chaps, but I suppose they have a point.

ISAAC VIVIAN ALEXANDER RICHARDS 1971–

Career Figures:	Innings 357	Runs 16,082	Average 48.00
Tests (36):	Innings 57	Runs 3,265	Average 59.36

C L WALCOTT

WEST INDIES

Walcott is the name. In the 1958 *Wisden*, Norman Preston wrote: 'When in 1951 *Wisden* paid tribute to F. M. Worrell and Everton Weekes, the Editor remarked in his preface: "my only regret was that room could not be found for C. L. Walcott." Now the opportunity is taken to include the third member of the famous W triumvirate, all of whom first saw the light of day on that lovely sunny island of Barbados . . .'

Later on, Preston leaves the sunshine alone, and gets down to the batting (and a bit of fielding and wicket-keeping). 'Standing six feet two inches and turning the scales at fifteen stone (now he is slightly heavier) Walcott has a commanding presence on and off the field.' I must confess that I like the 'slightly heavier' touch. But then, Preston gets down to the technical stuff. 'His powerful physique enables him to drive with tremendous force. He has a peerless off-drive, and a dazzling square cut, and is no less adept with the pull and hook, so that on his day he is rarely lost for a stroke . . .'

Well, yes, I would subscribe to that. But when you are not 'on your day' it's a different kettle of fish. A first-class footballer can, in the course of ninety minutes miss two open goals, two penalties, and then win the game with a goal in injury time. First-class batsmen have a bit of luck, now and then, but more often than not they are dismissed cheaply (even shabbily at times) without the caution, the yellow card, and the red card. When you're out, you're out. Just get walking, and a very long walk it is. When you are out for a duck, the members of Lord's may feel for you but they do not rise in acclaim, nor do you raise your bat in appreciation. It is a dismal business, but you get used to it. There's nothing like a nice, nippy ninety in, say, the second innings, to restore the spirits.

As always, Mr C. L. R. James brings his own special touch to the proceedings. You must keep your eye open for the revealing phrase (rather like the unusual shot or the crucial occasion when an innings is dominated and a series won). 'Walcott,' writes James in *The World of Cricket*, 'started the

1957 season in England in splendid form but injured himself in the first Test when scoring 90. Never afterwards did he recapture form and, though he ended the season with good figures, yet his past achievements and commanding style when he did make runs left a feeling of some massive piece of machinery gone wrong . . .'

There was something brutal about the man and about his batting which was immediately evident. Of the three Ws he clearly hit the ball the hardest, as Brian Statham will vouch if you ask him about a day at Sabina Park when the ball was repeatedly cannoned back past him, only to bounce back so far from the solid concrete sightscreen that he could simply pick it up again as he walked back for his next ball. What added to this impression of a doughty opponent was the serious and somewhat impassive countenance which he showed to the world. Whereas Weekes would flash a ready smile and Worrell might find time for a chat, Walcott was all business.

If we remember Weekes for the flashing square cut and Worrell for the elegantly-timed cover drive, then we should remember Walcott for the thumping hit of the overpitched ball, either through the covers or preferably straight back past the bowler, making him hop out of the way. This was not the Hammond-like swing with the front foot placed and poised to the pitch of the ball, but hit more firm-footed with an arch of the back and a bulge of muscle from the top of his head to the tip of his toes. I had misgivings about separating him from the West Indian threesome, and thought of placing him among the heavy brigade, but raw power was his trademark and set him clearly apart.

CLYDE LEOPOLD WALCOTT OBE 1941–1963

Career Figures:	Innings 238	Runs 11,820	Average 56.55
Tests (44):	Innings 74	Runs 3,798	Average 56.68

SUPREMOS

G. S. CHAPPELL
I. M. CHAPPELL
M. C. COWDREY
S. M. GAVASKAR
A. L. HASSETT
S. J. McCABE
J. H. W. FINGLETON
R. G. POLLOCK
E. de C. WEEKES

In batting terms, these are the men who have the batting art worked out, fully understood and can be relied on over a period to score runs in virtually any circumstances.

A hundred runs was the minimum target for any of these players, and once they had settled in and scored the first 20 or 30, there was no earthly reason, no normal human intervention, which could disturb their progress. That is not to say they were above petty error or even the occasional foolish stroke but such things were not an essential part of their make-up.

Scoring, to the likes of Gavaskar, Weekes and Pollock is an activity which continues from month to month in a steady flow. Why hurry things now when there is always another hour to come or another day or another week when the same problems can be solved and the business of batting continued?

Ian Chappell may fit this category a little less comfortably than his young brother, Greg, but he was no less successful in terms of results and I see him neither as an artist, nor as a strongman.

Cowdrey is perhaps the man I have most in mind in this category. His name is synonymous with steady accumulation of batting honours, thoughtful, stylish and accomplished. Yet, as I write the words, it makes me wonder why Graveney is not represented in this category and, no doubt, other personal favourites of the reader.

The trouble is that picking these names is more about who to leave out than who to include. My list is approximately forty out of the hundreds of superb players spanning the period. Graveney was not the artist I have in mind when I think of Arthur Morris or Denis Compton. Graveney had an interrupted and not altogether successful Test career. He just misses the boat. Anyway he gets a large mention here, which must show something of my guilt in leaving him on the quayside.

G S CHAPPELL
I M CHAPPELL

AUSTRALIA

Some might think it strange that two brothers could be so very different as batsmen. As a younger brother myself, I would hazard the suggestion that Greg Chappell, a strong character in his own right, needed to assert his own nature by playing, however subconsciously, differently from big brother Ian.

If one or the other is to rate highly with the great technical masters of the game, it is Greg. Ian has always been too much of a back foot player, and is therefore much too square-on for the purists. Greg has been too much of a front foot player to satisfy some criteria, and in his early days was so predominantly a hitter on the leg side that it seemed he would never be more than a make-weight at Test level.

If anyone felt that these deficiencies might stop the purposeful brothers from going their own way to the top in Test cricket, they were soon to be proved very wrong. Ian, the more obviously and outwardly aggressive of the two, made his mark by his strength, athleticism, eye for the ball, and an ability to play at his best when things were most against him. He was an exceptional player of slow bowling, mainly because he accorded it little or no respect, whatever the state of the game or the pitch. More than most he handed out stick to orthodox left arm bowling, hitting it to leg: and to orthodox off-spin, crashing it to the off-side.

Going back to Greg's initial strength on the leg side, it was quite uncanny that he could time the ball so well in that area; on the half volley, off a length, and short of a length, off his legs, and off his hip. I wrote as a journalist on Illingworth's tour to Australia, when Greg scored his maiden Test hundred at Perth, that no single stroke since the famous Compton Sweep had so flummoxed the bowlers and exercised the minds of the tacticians in the England side. That there was a resilience and a willingness to learn and change in Greg was soon apparent, because the combined thinking of the England on a new tactical approach proved singularly ineffective. The line of the attack was shifted to the off-side, but Greg's facility to score on that side of the wicket responded accordingly.

Maybe it was because of Ian's success that everyone was always taking a sideways look at the young brother to see if he would measure up. It seemed that Greg always had something to prove. He came to England and learned some of his cricket down at Somerset, and I remember him, with a growing reputation, playing at Hove for the first time.

Now it was just this kind of young budding cricketer whom the England fast bowler of the time, the stormy John Snow, would usually make it his business to teach a short, sharp and salutary lesson. Greg was not to avoid these attentions of Snow's, who produced a very quick, very straight, perfectly angled bouncer which cracked the poor lad on the head and summarily removed him from the field of battle. It says much for Greg's determination and courage that this savage blow seemed to have little or no effect on his subsequent play of quick bowling, which has been exemplary.

The 1973 *Wisden*, after noting Greg's experience of English conditions when playing for Somerset in the 1968 and 1969 seasons observes: 'There was a time when Greg Chappell was so strong on the onside that it was considered poor form not to concentrate round about his off stump and induce the edged chance to the wicket-keeper or slip. In the space of twelve months all that has changed. Critics watching his performance against the Rest of the World in the international matches compared him favourably with some of the great players over the years in Australian first-class cricket . . . He is one of the new young breed of Australian cricketers who have the intense desire to see Australia back on top in international cricket.'

Well Mr Packer shook things up rather violently since then and there are now problems in the field of cricket that have nothing to do with those on the cricket field. It may well be that Mr Packer's 'Australian' initiative did not stem – but rather released – the potential of first-class cricketers throughout the world. We can only wait on events.

As for Greg's batting, it is best remembered, in England, for his performance in the 1972 tour when, according to *Wisden*, he confirmed his place as Australia's number one batsman, hitting four centuries, three half-centuries and scoring 1,260 runs in 17 innings. The highlight was the Lord's Test when he scored 131 against some good quick bowling, 'from the technical and concentration point of view, it was perhaps the innings he most enjoyed in his cricket career.'

In contrast, fast bowling has had a fair share of success against Ian who, at one stage, lost his ability for the hook shot. What replaced it was a remarkably ungainly squatting down, with the bat left, ludicrously, pointing skywards like some submarine periscope which the ball might strike on its way through.

G S/I M CHAPPELL

Greg (left) and Ian Chappell (right) have made a remarkable impact on cricket over the last fifteen years. Despite being brothers, their batting styles are far apart: Ian is very much a back-foot player and an exceptional destroyer of slow bowling; Greg prefers to play off the front foot and is excellent at playing fast bowling.

Thinking more about this particular problem strengthens my contention that the square-on player will always have problems with the short, fast rising ball, unless he is a consummate and consistent hooker. He provides too big a target, which means that moving sideways out of the way takes too long. Therefore the only thing to do is to bob down from the waist, ducking towards the ball. This is a particularly dangerous occupation if the ball doesn't get up as high as expected.

It should be remembered that Ian went into retirement only to reappear on the scene with Kerry Packer's World Series cricket. The World Series Cricket Managing Director at the time, Andrew Caro, in his book *With A Straight Bat*, had this to say about Ian Chappell: 'Despite all his personal faults, which relate mainly to behaviour and etiquette, and reflect a social rebelliousness which is infuriating, Ian is straight and honest . . . There is a touch of schizophrenia in his behaviour. One moment he is helpful, cooperative and a pleasure to work with: the next he is an angry, irrational martinet . . . Over and above his batting and his bowling, there was his contribution as captain: he was undoubtedly the best captain in World Series Cricket. Not only was he more astute tactically, he also was unmatched in leadership qualities which made the Australian team both devoted and united. If there was a happy side in World Series Cricket it was the Australians.'

Ian scored ten centuries in his first fifty Test matches, and in 1971 succeeded Lawry as captain of Australia. He was a militant player and articulate with it – hence, perhaps, those outbreaks of 'bad language'. But he was prepared to listen to sound advice (from certain quarters), particularly about that hooking problem. In the 1970–1971 season, Sir Donald Bradman had a word in his ear. 'He said,' writes Chappell: '"You used to be a good hooker . . . what's happened to that shot?" It was time I reintroduced the hook shot to my range.'

His approach was always very strong, very positive. 'At the crease my attitude towards bouncers has been that if I'm playing well enough, three bouncers an over should be worth twelve runs to me.'

Then there was Greg Chappell, the Australian captain who ploughed his way through a difficult assignment in England when news broke of the complete team defection to Packer, resulting in such disruption that a goodish side was comprehensively beaten. Meanwhile, Greg kept his cool and his own playing standards high while all around him were failing miserably.

Later, when the rift between the World Series Cricket and traditional Test cricket run by the Board was healed in Australia in 1979–80, it was Greg who took over the reins and showed himself to be an effective and useful leader in difficult times, dealing with the outbursts of his elders, Denis Lillee and brother Ian, with considerable tact and determination. They were quite a handful, those two grandsons of the late former Australian cricketer Vic Richardson, but they were a gutsy pair who made significant contributions to Australian cricket in a period of change which was by no means entirely of their own making.

GREGORY STEPHEN CHAPPELL 1966–

Career Figures:	Innings 455	Runs 20,435	Average 51.99
Tests (61):	Innings 109	Runs 5,171	Average 55.01

IAN MICHAEL CHAPPELL 1961–1980

Career Figures:	Innings 448	Runs 19,680	Average 48.35
Tests (75):	Innings 136	Runs 5,345	Average 42.42

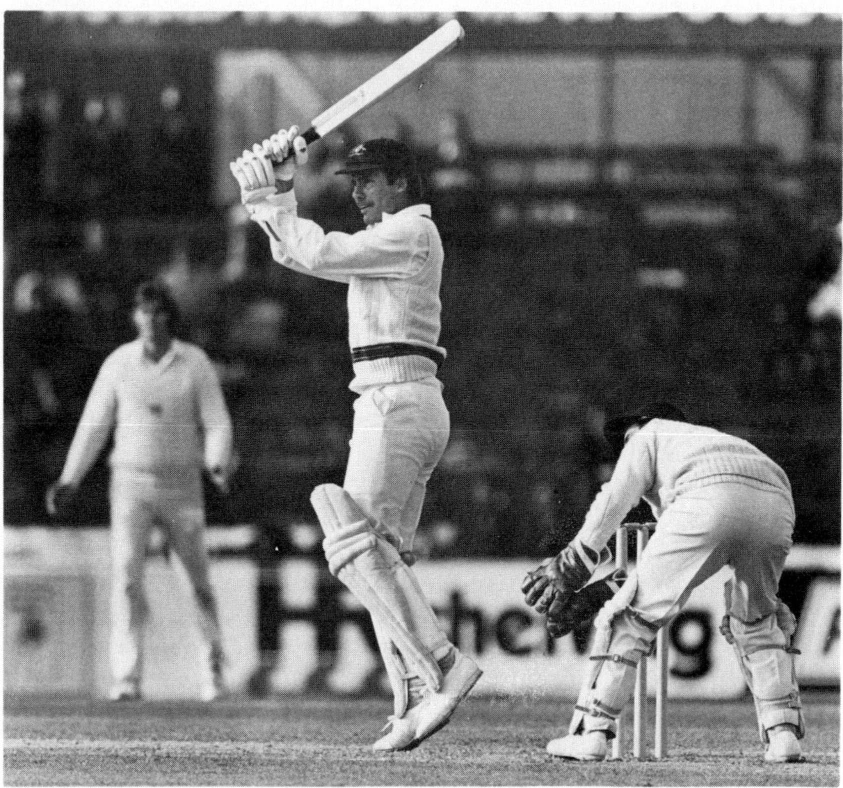

Greg Chappell's initial strength lay in his uncanny timing of any ball on the leg side. This particular shot he has made all his own.

M C COWDREY

ENGLAND

Now we have Cowdrey, a true contemporary of mine indeed, described as 'cricketer for England, Oxford University, and Kent. A boy prodigy, and England Batsman at 22.' Taking another leaf from the same book, we have Dexter, 'cricketer for England, Cambridge University, and Sussex . . . an exciting batsman, one of the few to rate comparison with those of cricket's Golden Age before the First World War. He seemed to fear no bowler, and often paid for this indifference.'

Well yes, that's about right, but what of Colin Cowdrey, a master batsman and a man in the slips for all bowlers? When you have known and played with and against him (interminably I sometimes feel) and even liked him into the bargain, it's difficult to get the judgement right. These are my personal impressions of the cricketer and the man.

The reason Colin was called Kipper had more to do with sleep than with fish. Throughout his playing career he was always on the heavy side and trying to avoid getting any heavier. When continually active, as in the middle of a cricket season or on tour, he found that any unnecessary activity, while he was eating less than he wanted, left him unduly tired. So when not actually on the field he preferred to rest up in bed.

If you had to pick one facet of his batting, which singled him out from all the others I have seen, it would be the impression of having so much time in which to play. Of course this is what sets one batsman above another, the infallible sign of a great player; but I must remind you that I am speaking of Colin Cowdrey, not simply among his contemporaries, but in the company of batsmen of four or five decades, and I mean that to be as sizeable a compliment as it sounds.

When people criticised Cowdrey for occasionally slipping into the doldrums, in a swirling sea which lacked all motive force, they may not have realised the extent to which all his batting was a matter of pre-consideration, the thought process comfortably preceding the physical action. He told me quite recently of the incredibly fine pitch to which he tuned mind and body in his search for the complete answer to every ball, every bowler, and every situation. 'It is easy to lose the thread', he said, 'such as when you clip a leg stump half volley for what inside you seems to be a certain four, and it turns out to be a comfortable piece of fielding practice for mid on. Then you do it again and start to wonder what has gone wrong with the system. In no time at all you are reconsidering the whole basis of your legside play and all intuitive reaction to the ball is extinguished for the time being.' If I had a criticism of Cowdrey's cricketing career, it would be that he seemed to find it harder than many to come to a definite decision. This problem was with him in his batting, in his captaincy, and in his relationships with other players. It may be that his complicated thought process left him weighing up the two, or three, or even more possibilities, so that he dallied while pondering the alternatives. Certainly of the batsmen with whom I have played he was infinitely capable of more than one stroke to any given ball, and that in itself must lead to an occasional sense of confusion. But given a clear brief, a clear mind, or whatever was needed to unleash the great Cowdrey gift in a single unalterable direction, he had few peers in the art of putting bat to ball. Rightly or wrongly I take credit for one of these occasions.

A master batsman, and a superb fielder in the slips, Colin Cowdrey played in 114 Test matches. He is the only cricketer to have represented his country on more than a hundred occasions and, as well as sharing in five record batting partnerships, he held more Test catches (120) than any other fielder, excluding wicket-keepers.

As we walked out to bat against the massed ranks of the West Indies fast bowlers at Port of Spain, Trinidad, he very much the senior player, I on my first full tour, I ventured the opinion that we should not be too long in taking the initiative or else we would be nothing more than Aunt Sallies. A lift of the eyebrow and a slight nod of the head was all the information I had to go on, but, once battle was joined, it was soon clear that I had struck a responsive chord. I thought I played pretty well myself that morning with 40 or 50 runs on the board, but all the while Colin made me look like a selling-plater, and he was well in the 60s or 70s by the time the interval came. Even though we had faced almost exclusively fast bowling, which was my forte, he had left me in no doubt as to who was boss.

In his book *The Greatest of My Time*, Trevor Bailey writes: 'There have been occasions when I have bowled against him [Cowdrey] for Essex when he has been almost unrecognisable. He has scratched and pottered around against mediocre bowling, making batting appear an extremely laboured business . . .' Yes, my dear Trevor, you can say that again, once more with feeling. Bailey's character analysis of Cowdrey is admirable, shrewd and very funny. And he concludes: 'Personally, I shall be indebted to him, not only for the pleasure of playing with and against him, but because his presence has invariably helped to make the game itself all the more enjoyable . . .'

In *MCC: the Autobiography of a Cricketer*, Cowdrey wrote about Bradman: 'He came nearer to mastering the art of batsmanship than anyone. He had astonishing fleetness of foot, sharpness of eye and timing, but it was his mind that powered his success.' Cowdrey was also under the influence of Hutton. He recalls a game at Scarborough: 'I was fielding in the deep those days, and so I had time to watch and analyse this fabulous automaton throughout his innings. He was always in balance. When he played forward his head, his left knee and front toe were always in perfect, text-book position. Nothing seemed more certain than that he would go on making hundreds . . . I became a total disciple of the way he played. My temperament was adjusted to his method as opposed, say, to the methods of Ted Dexter and Graeme Pollock in later years.'

Disciples seldom attain the stature of their masters as Cowdrey undoubtedly has. It would be a tough choice, Hutton or Cowdrey, at any team selection meeting, wouldn't it?

MICHAEL COLIN COWDREY CBE 1950–1976

Career Figures:	Innings 1,130	Runs 42,719	Average 42.89
Tests (114):	Innings 188	Runs 7,624	Average 44.06

S M GAVASKAR

INDIA

Sunil Gavaskar stands five foot five inches high, about the same size as Napoleon. Although he never conquered Europe or invaded Russia, Gavaskar has persistently wrought havoc at the crease. And if there is a single part of his batting style which accounts for consistent success against the strongest attacks in the world, it is the 'straightness' of his bat.

Now that may seem the most elementary requirement for any good player, but it is surprising how few manage to show the full face of the blade hanging down in a perfect perpendicular. The ability to do so gives rise to the most coveted compliment amongst connoisseurs of batting, which can be applied unstintingly to 'Sonny' Gavaskar, i.e. he has the broadest bat in the game.

The broad bat phenomenon is hard to pin down. It does not necessarily belong exclusively to the stonewall, defensive brigade, nor is it necessarily the trademark of batsmen who seldom get the bat out of the vertical and into the horizontal plane. Geoff Boycott, for instance, would not be considered a 'broad bat' man, and neither would Neil Harvey nor Colin Milburn, for all their individual brilliance.

There may be a slight prejudice in favour of very small men whose full size bats simply look bigger in contrast to their small stature. Hanif Mohammad for instance would qualify for this category, but even this piece of logic fails to explain the whole story. It is a simple fact that some batsmen make more of their bat than others.

Perhaps the broadest bat of my time, and I fancy that most of my generation would agree with me, belonged to Peter May. There were times when, for the bowler, it seemed as though he had the proverbial barn door in his hand. I don't know whether any suspicious blighter ever had the temerity to measure across the face of May's bat; hundreds must have been tempted, and when a man could make a maximum width of 4¼ inches (10.8 centimetres) look like double, then who could blame them. After May, a big broad man himself, I would be happy to nominate Gavaskar as next in line.

Gavaskar was born in Bombay, in 1949: his uncle M. K. Mandri had kept wicket for Bombay and India. Certainly there are some impressive facts and figures in Gavaskar's career. On India's tour of England in 1979, Gavaskar played in all four Tests for an average of 77.42. In the last Test at The Oval, India, set to make 438 and so to win the game, failed to do so by only nine runs. It was Gavaskar again. He stayed put for over eight hours for 221 runs.

The great shame about that magnificent innings was that it only earned India a draw, when the winning of a memorable Test match was there for the taking. The Indians can point to a sudden rash of umpiring decisions against them for their sudden loss of impetus, but they must know in their hearts that they lost the match by keeping back their next best batsman, Viswanath when ten minutes in the middle with Gavaskar must surely have brought the prize they so richly deserved.

The 1980 *Wisden* records: 'When he sets his sights high, he builds his innings with meticulous craftsmanship, limiting himself to the strokes he knows best – drives through the covers, past the bowler, and between mid-on and mid-wicket. But when he lets his hair down, his range of shots and the power behind them are quite astonishing.'

Gavaskar was the first Indian to score over 700 runs in a Test series, and the first ever Test player to score over 700 runs in a debut Test series. But there were some problems. I can do no better than quote K. N. Prabhu on Gavaskar in *The Cricketer*, July 1971. After a successful transition through schools, colleges, and University cricket, 'he learnt that cricket would be a game of ups and downs, that it could be hard going at the highest levels.' So he got down to some homework, toured the West Indies, and, in the first and second Tests, made 65 and 116 – with Sobers of all people failing to gather easy catches early in both innings.

Prabhu goes on with some discerning and qualified comments: 'His tall scores are apt to give the impression that he is a lovely and venturesome batsman. This would not be a strictly accurate picture. Gavaskar is not the gay cavalier that Engineer is; he is also not one of the dull dogs . . . he is the sort of batsman who is likely to be appreciated in Yorkshire no less than in Kent . . . he has a thumping square drive and the ability and willingness to advance on quick feet to attack the spinners – factors which should please the discerning follower of cricket.'

The other problem which has affected Gavaskar's career is the same problem which seems to dog Indian Test cricket as a whole, i.e. problems over leadership. Whereas in England the hiring and firing of captains may be overinfluenced by the media, in India it seems to be unduly governed by internal political considerations amongst the administrators.

The Nawab of Pataudi (the younger) seemed a natural and effective leader, and yet the job soon passed to apparently lesser individuals. The same has happened to Gavaskar. Here is a man with the drive to make things happen, and the character to engage the cooperation of his team-mates, but those terms of captaincy have been abruptly cut short for no apparent reason. The effect on Gavaskar the batsman has been noticeable when he returned to the ranks. A certain disinterested air creeps into his normally assertive attitude, and it is a tribute to his basic concern for Indian cricket, and to his own standards, that he has continued to get his head down when it matters.

Nowhere was this more conspicuous than on the 1979 tour in England. Following the team round in the early summer, I saw any amount of fancy strokes from Gavaskar, but it was not until the eve of the First Test that he took the trouble to take a hundred off Hampshire. Then in the Tests, he was not quite convincing for a while – when Gavaskar is not quite 'right' it is usually loose play outside off-stump that tells the tale – but as the series wore on and his services became of increasing importance to the team, so his resolve visibly hardened, leading up to that magnificent 221 runs at The Oval. Gavaskar sent a lot of people home happy on the two days of that memorable innings – his hundred, his double hundred. When you remember that he has barely had an easy series in his life, always playing against England, Australia and West Indies, it is a superb record.

SUNIL MANOHAR GAVASKAR 1966–

Career Figures:	Innings 388	Runs 17,712	Average 50.89
Tests (63):	Innings 114	Runs 5,974	Average 56.35

A L HASSETT

AUSTRALIA

Lindsay Hassett played in forty-three Test matches for Australia, twenty-four as captain. He took over the job from Bradman and when he retired had scored fifty-nine centuries in first-class cricket. That awful shadow of the Don never seemed to bother him much. 'Standing only five feet five inches, he was probably the most brilliant batsman of his size the world has ever seen. . . Nor was it only the small man's strokes he possessed, the hook, the cut, the quick-footed drive; he could force the good length ball in front of the wicket and never get underneath it. Even at his most defensive, he was always perfectly balanced and always made batting look easy. The number of runs he made was astonishing; when he retired, only Bradman among Australians had scored more hundreds.'

Physical height is a vital factor in the art of batting. Traditionally, the very tall men are front foot drivers, whereas the little titches make do with cuts, pulls, and deflections. Exceptions would be Frank Woolley for the tall brigade; he was a splendid puller and hooker of the short ball, and perhaps Hassett represents the small men as one who was unwilling to accept the limitations of his stature, and played an all-round game without difficulty. Nevertheless, the old adage that 'a good big un' beats a good little un' probably holds good. Whereas the big man who doesn't hook can probably cope, the rising ball to the shorter fellow, who is not in a position to play a cross-bat stroke, obviously brings considerable problems. An intriguing attempt to deal with this was developed by England wicket-keeper and highly effective lower order batsman, Alan Knott. By placing the top hand, i.e., being a right-hander, his left hand, round the back of the bat handle, he claimed, and to an extent proved, he could play very high in defence – right up in front of his face, which the classic left-hand position does not allow.

Personally I take the view that as the difference in height is measured in so few inches – which represents a very small percentage difference of overall

A L HASSETT

Despite being a short man, Lindsay Hassett played an all-round game without difficulty. He was a brilliant batsman, combining elegance with boldness of stroke, and always made batting look easy. He was also an outstanding fielder.

height – too much is made of problems and advantages in this respect. It is probably born of the age-old social feelings of inferiority experienced by those of, for instance, five foot seven inches tall as opposed to those who top six foot. I can't think of any other situation where a difference of less than 10% can so radically affect attitudes. My advice to short and tall is to have no preconceived ideas about what they should or should not do.

The only genuine problem for the tall man is that to get down over his bat, his trunk, unless he has uncommonly long arms, is bent further over. This can put his head in a less than ideal position in relation to his feet. There is, of course, no restriction on the overall length of a bat and a specially long handle can be of assistance as long as the overall position does not become unwieldy. The only other piece of advice I tender to the tall man is not to overreach on the front foot. The time available is limited and greater height usually means less muscular speed rather than more. The tall man should expect only his front foot, except perhaps against slow bowling, to reach as far as the small man's, but he should remember the height advantage that this gives, keeping him well above the ball and allowing him to hit even the good length delivery in the sweet part of the bat.

Neville Cardus swooped on Hassett with delight and put the whole thing in proper historical perspective: 'It is bad criticism to set the masters of one period against those of another and to blame, say, a Hutton or a Hassett for not indulging the gestures and points of view of a MacLaren or a Jackson. MacLaren and Jackson were representative men in a particular national scene and atmosphere; Hutton and Hassett each are, in relation to the contemporary environment, equally representative. The style is the man himself. . . No great cricketer compromises his true character or his instinctive technical capacity. And if his technique doesn't work by instinct, he isn't a master. Hassett was born to natural elegance and boldness as a batsman; he found himself caught after 1939 in a tremendous transition, both in cricket and world environment . . . he never lost lightness of touch, though, no matter how, for the cause's sake, he controlled himself, but in hand, often seeming to hide himself behind it, over after over. . . He played cricket with the wit of his mind.'

Hassett, the man with the dry wit and laconic asides has always seemed to draw lyrical responses from his critics. Denzil Batchelor in 1952: 'At his very best as a batsman, Hassett had more elegance than any other Australian in the post-Kippax era: moreover he was a run-getter in the high Australian fashion – no mere maker of magic passes south of the wicket. His 33 at Leeds in 1938 when Bill Bowes was bowling like a Prince of Darkness had most to do with Australia winning that crucial Test match. . . It has always been worth watching even the dourest Test match sleepwalking its way to the everlasting bonfire, to gaze on Hassett cutting off boundaries in the deep. He skims the perimeter with the noiseless speed of a water-beetle.' Just so, his fielding was in the same class as his batting.

When Hassett lost the series to Hutton in England there was a view that he cared too little for the result and would have done better with a more concentrated, dour, and disciplinary approach. I doubt the truth of that – especially the premise that any Australian captain does not care deeply about winning or losing. My impression is that Hassett, like Sobers, was a man with cricket in his bones, who put the game first, above its politics, above petty loyalties, and above jingoism. We should all be grateful for that.

ARTHUR LINDSAY HASSETT MBE 1932–1953

Career Figures:	Innings	322	Runs	16,890	Average	58.24
Tests (43):	Innings	69	Runs	3,073	Average	46.56

S J McCABE
J H W FINGLETON

AUSTRALIA

I make no apology for linking two great names in Australian cricket. They clearly deserve individual comment and have certainly received it at length from other writers and critics. However, I never saw McCabe play and have only still photographs to go on, and the same is true of Fingleton. They played in the same team, and, despite their contrasting styles, they seem to make bedfellows of a kind, however reluctant.

What I do know is that if Don Bradman wanted to watch him, then McCabe must have been some player. As for Fingleton, for me he was a regular and doughty golfing partner to while away the off duty hours on the Illingworth tour to Australia which I covered for the *Sunday Mirror*, and he was a welcome guest at a happy evening at my home when he was relaxed enough to remove his shoes which were killing him and to take off his socks to cool his toes! Anyway, the fact is that most people in the press box are always interested to hear what Fingleton has to say, and that is praise enough. But let us start with McCabe.

A remarkable, almost unknown, Indian writer, aged seventeen, wrote a book *Cricket Cavalcade*, published in 1976. His name is Mahiyar Morawalla and he wrote: 'If given the choice, I would play cricket all round the clock to the end of my life. That failing, I would like to read about cricket.' And that he certainly must have done, with skill, love, and industry. Wherever he did his research, he's very good on McCabe.

'In the 1930s Stan McCabe was Australia's most dashing batsman. He played in a side which contained the redoubtable Bradman, the dour Jack Fingleton, the prolific Ponsford and the "unbowlable" Woodfull – yet he was able to hold his own in such a company of outstanding batsmen . . . He regarded cricket, even Test cricket, as a game to be played for pleasure and enjoyment . . . In his murderous mood he was irrepressible. When in full flow, his batting was more brilliant, more intrepid, more vigorous, and more attractive than even Don Bradman's. His bat was a trenchant sword, eagerly routing the foe, dominating the situation, and reducing the best bowlers to impotency.' Well, nobody ever said that about Jack Fingleton, just as they never said it about Trevor Bailey, Geoffrey Boycott, or Hanif Mohammad.

For sure, this lyrical, romantic appreciation has its origins more in reading than in playing. For a more austere, technical analysis, we must go back again to *The World of Cricket*: 'In his prime McCabe was of medium size, well-knit, strong and extremely agile. His stance was nicely balanced, and the bat came down from exactly over the middle stump. He was a fine player of all types of bowling but excelled against pace. Perfect reflexes, and the fact that his weight was evenly distributed on either foot, enabled him, when faced by the greatest fast bowlers of his day, to drive the overpitched ball without losing the ability to position himself for the hook when necessary, a talent confined to the highest class of batsmen.'

Clearly he was in the highest class. Just take three innings: 'At Sydney, in 1932–33, he rallied a side, nonplussed by the full fury of Larwood with 187 not out. In South Africa, in 1835–36, he scored 189, again not out, and in 1938, at Trent Bridge, he scored 232 . . . This was the occasion when 'Bradman exhored his team not to miss a ball of this batting for, he said, never again would they see the like.' It could be said that since 1938 (and I'm sure Bradman would agree) that just as great – if not greater – innings have been played in Test cricket, even at Trent Bridge, but I can't be certain as I wasn't there. McCabe was born in 1910. The evidence is plain enough, though, that he must have been one of the greatest batsmen of his time.

Greatest batsman, greatest bowler, greatest all-rounder, greatest wicket-keeper, greatest fielder – the choice is wide and opinions vary a mile. But there are not so many cricketers/journalists who can honestly claim equal skill with bat and pen. In fact in Jack Fingleton's case, the written word has long since typified the man and dimmed the memory of him as a player.

Denzil Batchelor commented: 'To write about cricket, you need the pinpointing accuracy of a map-maker, the prophetic gift of Nostradamus, the forthrightness of Hazlitt, the lapidary Roman quality and the profound imagery of Sir Thomas Browne, the energy and skill in manoeuvre of a polo pony, and the patience in affliction of Job himself.' That bit about Job himself is certainly apt when you read this by Ian Johnson: 'The impression of present-day cricketers in Australia, and I think it is a unanimous opinion', said Johnson, 'is that Bill O'Reilly and Jack Fingleton are doing more harm than most to the game . . . They have made absolutely no effort to be constructive. In fact, they have been entirely destructive.'

Part of Fingleton's cool response was this: 'If it could be shown that my writing and broadcasting had been calculated to destroy cricket, I would retire from such activities immediately because I love cricket – and owe much to it. In reality, I had always hoped that those who read me or listened to me would, as a result, be more interested in cricket.'

G. D. Martineau writes: 'Here, indeed, we have an unusual combination; at once a cricketer of high international quality and a literary critic, free from vulgarity and bias.' I agree about the literary ability and the absence of vulgarity, but I'm not to sure about the bias. Fingleton can be a very chauvinistic Australian when in the mood. But back to Martineau: 'Though not judged to be an attractive batsman of the McCabe type, he [Fingleton] was able on occasion to hit hard and score fast. He played many first-class innings, apart from those for which he is best known, and regularly helped both New South Wales and Australia by giving a good start.'

Quoting from Denzil Batchelor again: 'Fingleton first appeared on the scene against Jardine's team, and lasted till the war. He hit (or scraped, if you are violently prejudiced against him) a remarkable century against Allen's team at Brisbane, when no one else looked like a good batsman at all. He also helped to win the final decisive Test with a big innings.' As you can see there seem to be lingering doubts about whether Fingleton was a great and entertaining batsman. But, as a reporter, his sharpness of phrase and acute perceptions have, without doubt, enriched the history of the game, both in broadcasting and writing – especially the latter.

STANLEY JOSEPH McCABE 1928–1942

Career Figures:	Innings 262	Runs 11,951	Average 49.38
Tests (39):	Innings 62	Runs 2,748	Average 48.21

JOHN HENRY WEBB FINGLETON OBE 1930–1940

Career Figures:	Innings 166	Runs 6,816	Average 44.54
Tests (18):	Innings 29	Runs 1,189	Average 42.46

R G POLLOCK

SOUTH AFRICA

Sport and politics; are they indivisible? This is not the time to go into this knotty problem but I quote from Louis Duffus on Graeme Pollock. He was 'in his prime when political factors led to the cancellations of the MCC tour of 1967–68 to South Africa and he, like many others of both countries, was denied the opportunity of appearing in a series which promised infinite delights.' This was the tragic side of this mighty player's career.

On the plus side, however, Graeme had the pleasure of being warmly, even ecstatically, appreciated by players and journalists alike. See Michael Melford, *The Cricketer* 1970: 'This is the age of competence and solid application rather than of genius and magic, so the presence of Graeme Pollock among the world's great batsmen is all the more striking . . . The power and range of his strokes and the grandeur of some of his most famous innings have confirmed him as a batsman who would have adorned any age.' Graeme Pollock had one outstanding trait in his stroke play which set him apart, if not above, all his contemporaries and possibly apart from every other batsman.

His forte, or possibly his unique contribution to the art of batting, was that he could hit the good length ball, given only a modicum of room outside the off-stump, actually harder than he could hit the half volley. Now that takes some doing and it is worth studying Pollock's style to understand how he did it.

He was, in fact, studiously correct, staying firmly sideways in his defensive strokes, and he reaped the benefit of this splendid body position when it came to attacking the ball on the rise. Of course, he was a very tall man, certainly over six feet two inches and he stood his full height, as of course you have to do to hit the ball on the rise. There can be no better illustration of this technique than that which came at Trent Bridge in 1965 when he hit 125 runs off a supposedly tight typical England seam attack, with the least possible difficulty. And it is those devastating strokes played through cover

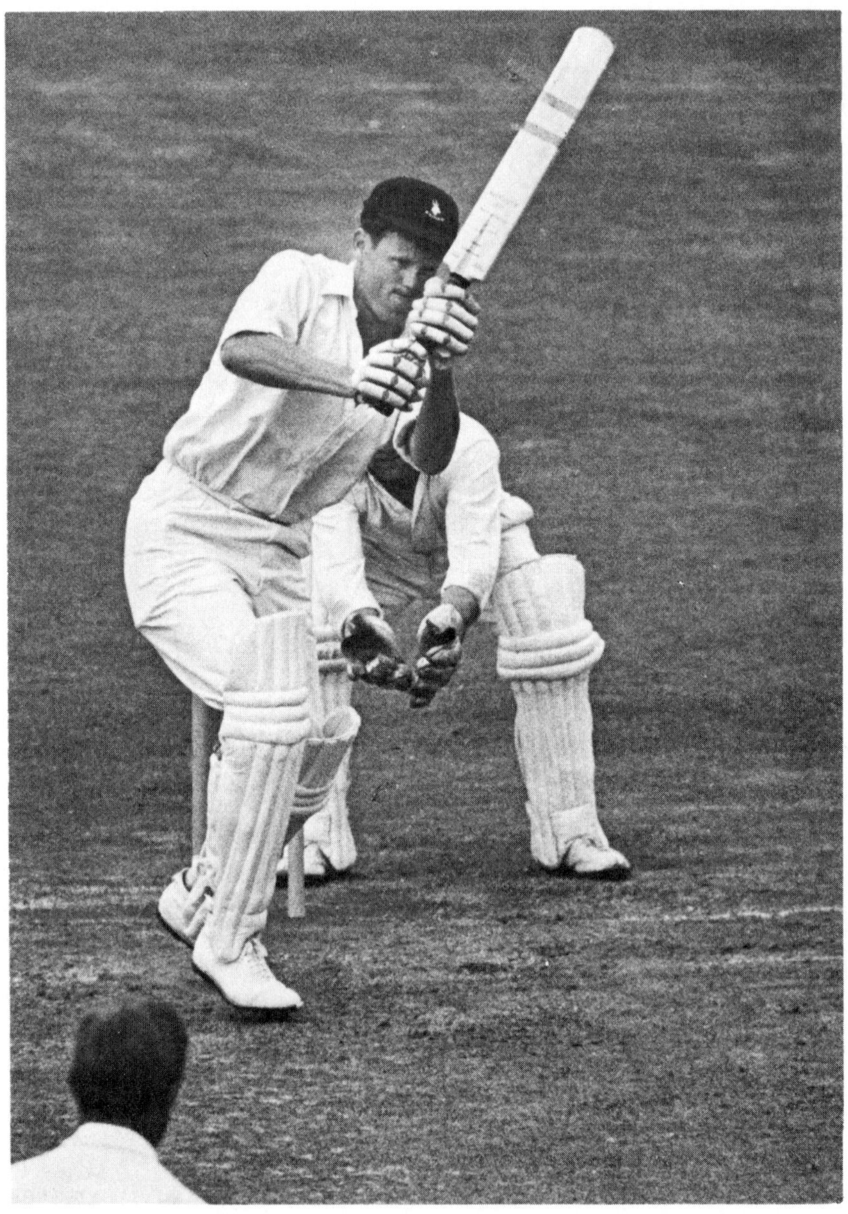

Graeme Pollock's stroke-play was majestic. He had a complete range of strokes and executed them with considerable power, no more so than when playing genuine good length balls through the covers off either the front or back foot.

and extra cover off both front and back foot off a genuine good length that stick in my memory.

Strangely, it was this very orthodox, almost exaggeratedly orthodox, positioning which initially gave bowlers encouragement to think there were ways of getting him out or perhaps tying him down. I remember England's first major encounter with the man on the tour to South Africa, 1964–65, when the slow bowlers, particularly Fred Titmus, thought that his sideways positioning could lead him into trouble with the off spinner bowling round the wicket and running the ball on towards the leg side. Indeed, they did have one or two successes, moral and actual. But what in fact proved to be his more than adequate defence against this probing, was a splendid judgement of length. He wasn't to be tempted forward when the ball wasn't there to play, and, in fact, I would rate him alongside Gary Sobers in his ability to pick the slightly short-of-the-length ball from the slow bowler and to hit it straight bat, high and wide of mid on, as often as not for six.

There was also a theory, because he was mainly a straight bat player as opposed to a cross bat player – getting the bat out of the vertical into the horizontal plane – that he would have trouble with the faster bowlers. On that tour in South Africa, John Price of Middlesex was our fastest – but not perhaps the ideally aggressive type of bowler to exploit that particular weakness, if indeed it was one. I suppose again it was his height and judgement of length which enabled him to survive quite comfortably against some pretty fast bowling from time to time; and bowling generally had only to be a fraction sub-standard to prompt the full majestic flow of his stroke play.

His technique was sufficiently studied to make you feel that he had been the subject of a good deal of instruction as a lad. He thought and talked technique a good deal and was certainly willing to experiment also. I remember particularly when he was playing for the International Cavaliers in England, who were the pioneers of the Sunday afternoon forty-overs cricket, when he divulged that he really felt that footwork was largely unnecessary as long as one spread one's feet eighteen inches or so and simply rocked onto the back one for the back foot shot and leaned over the front one for the front foot shot. Again, it may be because of his height and erect attitude that this system seemed to work for him, although I suspect that it was more successful against Sunday afternoon bowling than it would have been in a Test match. I certainly remember him using his feet more positively in one or two of the limited number of Test match innings in which I was privileged to watch him play.

I have one other abiding, and indeed infuriating, memory of him, which was in his capacity as a bowler. He was an occasional leg spin and googly bowler and it may seem odd that on this occasion he bowled the first over of the day in a Test match. The reason for this oddity was that Dexter had scored no fewer than 172 not out on the previous day, and had it very much in mind, on a beautiful pitch and a lightening outfield at Johannesburg, the Wanderers Ground, to repeat the performance the following day. It was a highly imaginative piece of captaincy to confront me the next morning with the last bowler I would have expected, Graeme Pollock. He pitched one in just the right spot and a hurried defensive stroke simply nicked in to the wicketkeeper. So 172 not out one day, 172 out in the first over of the next. That is the kind of fate which deters cricketers from getting big ideas about themselves.

For all his massive scores, Pollock did have that old trouble of getting out cheaply of course. Take the 1963–64 tour of Australia: in the first match at Perth, Graham McKenzie got rid of him for 1 and 0. But on the return journey to Perth (after making 110 in a one-day country game) against a combined eleven he hit 127 not out in one hundred and eight minutes. Sir Donald Bradman is said to have remarked to Pollock afterwards: 'If you ever score a century like that again I hope I'll be there to see it.' And yet some critics have described him as 'a part-time genius'. He was accused of 'lacking in concentration' – that well-known phrase which reminds me of myself.

Going back to Pollock's childhood, Melford observes, 'there was mild concern in his family of talented games players when at the age of three he [Graeme] firmly gripped the bat left-handed, for he does everything else right-handed.' It is rather strange, but look at Denis Compton who batted right-handed and bowled left-handed for Middlesex and England, and played outside left for Arsenal and England when his dashes and cutting inside were followed by a cruel, devastating shot reminiscent of Cliff Bastin.

With his Test career truncated politically, Graeme Pollock remained a major force in Currie Cup cricket, scoring 1,000 runs in first-class matches as late as the 1975–76 winter. In *Wisden* he is linked in this performance with Barry Richards, 'these two provided the differences between genius and talent.'

ROBERT GRAEME POLLOCK 1960–

Career Figures:	Innings 335	Runs 16,460	Average 55.60
Tests (23):	Innings 41	Runs 2,256	Average 60.97

E de C WEEKES

WEST INDIES

Everton Weekes is very much of the Bailey period, and, certainly from an English point of view, Bailey writes with great authority about his batting. To begin with, most helpfully, he places Weekes nicely in context: 'Seldom, if ever, has one country – let alone a semi-tropical island, Barbados – possessed three middle order batsmen of the calibre of Weekes, Worrell and Walcott . . . yet they were not built alike, they did not look alike, and their cricketing methods were dissimilar . . . Weekes was a small, neat compact back-player, who possessed such a wonderful range of attacking strokes that bowling to him on a hard, fast, true wicket could be something of a nightmare. In addition he possessed a superb defence, and he was probably the most complete batsman of the three W's . . .' But, notes Bailey, 'there was sometimes a machine-like quality about Weeke's batting which reminded me of Sir Donald Bradman – a superlative run-getter, effective rather than beautiful.'

C. L. R. James, in *The World of Cricket* makes the same point as Bailey, 'Weekes is a batsman who for long periods attacked all bowlers in the same manner as Bradman . . . he excelled in fierce cuts and hooks off the faster bowlers and drove powerfully off either foot. He was not orthodox but would stand back to hit the length ball to the off or to the on. A defensive stroke often seemed a last improvisation to a ball which he had vainly planned to force away.'

Perhaps there's a hint of certain limitations here, but Weekes had a good record in England, was devastating in his own country and in India, but fallible in Australia where he was susceptible to the hook against a few (but fatal) bouncers from Lindwall and Miller – especially when that superb fielder Neil Harvey was standing on the deep square-leg boundary for that very reason. Weekes, it should be added, was another Lancashire League man, where, for a number of seasons, he achieved great success and popularity – and the invaluable experience of those 'bad' English wickets.

It is a matter of lasting regret that, whereas I saw plenty of Frank Worrell and enough of Clyde Walcott to form adequate judgements as to their style and ability, I never laid eyes on Weekes the batsman. Nor did he follow the steps of the other two into national administration, or Worrell to the captaincy, and Walcott into team management. Weekes mostly stayed at home and kept his straightforward humour and smiling face for those around him. So it must be an impression snatched here, a short conversation, or titbits gleaned from others, which form my picture of Weekes.

One such firm impression was gained while working with Weekes on the BBC television commentary team. There had been some indifferent cricket played by a famous player and many of us had tried to find excuses by using all sorts of euphemisms, i.e. 'not quite timing the ball' when we really meant 'determined apparently not to attempt to hit it' when the situation cried out

A powerful and sprightly batsman, Everton Weekes had a keen eye and extraordinary reflexes. He revelled in attacking the faster bowlers, many of whom suffered from his superb cutting and hooking.

for action. Not so Everton Weekes – although he never lost his smile and the gentle cadence of his normal speaking voice, he criticised strongly and when asked to consider mitigating factors, would not give one inch. In much I have read about Weekes' batting that trait stood him in good stead. Otherwise I see him as the true Caribbean buccaneer of the three Ws. The Errol Flynn with the flashing smile and the flashing blade, a sort of Rohan Kanhai and Basil Butcher rolled into one, with all these traits epitomised in his last great innings in England, that 90 at Lord's on a bad pitch, when he was hit badly more than once on the hands but cracked on while all around him were falling by the wayside. Even so, he was not entirely fit, and afterwards went back home to captain and coach Barbados.

With a Test average of 58.61 he only just failed to reach the immortal group of those who averaged 60.00 and above. I can only repeat my regret that I never saw him in full flow and have clearly missed a considerable experience.

EVERTON DE COURCY WEEKES OBE 1944–1964

Career Figures:	Innings 241	Runs 12,010	Average 52.90
Tests (48):	Innings 81	Runs 4,455	Average 58.61

ACKNOWLEDGEMENTS

I am particularly grateful to Clifford Makins who has collaborated with me on a number of books in the past and whose help in the researching and writing of this particular book was invaluable. I am also indebted to the following authors, literary agents, publishers, photographers and photographic libraries who have granted permission to reproduce copyright material.

EXTRACTS

John Arlott, Fred Trueman and Gilbert Phelps, *Arlott and Trueman on Cricket*, British Broadcasting Corporation, 1977
John Arlott (Editor), *The Oxford Companion to Sports and Games*, Oxford University Press, 1975
Trevor Bailey, *The Greatest of My Time*, Eyre & Spottiswoode, 1968
Ralph Barker, *Ten Great Innings*, Chatto & Windus, 1964
Denzil Batchelor, *The Book of Cricket*, Collins, 1952
Donald Bradman, *Farewell to Cricket*, Hodder & Stoughton, 1950
Ian Chappell, *Cricket in our Blood*, Stanley Paul, 1976
Denis Compton, *End of an Innings*, Oldbourne, 1958
Colin Cowdrey, *MCC: The Autobiography of a Cricketer*, Hodder & Stoughton, 1976
Ted Dexter, *Ted Dexter Declares*, Stanley Paul, 1966
Ernest Eytle, *Frank Worrell*, Hodder & Stoughton, 1963
Jack Fingleton, *Masters of Cricket*, Heinemann, 1958
Neil Harvey, *My World of Cricket*, Hodder & Stoughton, 1963
Reg Hayter (Editor), *Cricket: Stars of Today*, Pelham Books, 1973
Rachael Heyhoe Flint and Netta Rheinberg, *Fair Play: The Story of Women's Cricket*, Angus & Robertson (UK) Ltd, 1976
Leonard Hutton, *Just My Story*, Hutchinson, 1956
Bill Lawry, *Run-Digger*, Souvenir Press, 1966
Alan Lee, *A Pitch in Both Camps*, Stanley Paul, 1979
Rusi Modi, *Some Indian Cricketers*, National Book Trust, India, 1972
Mahiyar Morawalla, *Cricket Cavalcade*, Haico Publishing House, Bombay, 1976
A. G. Moyes, *A Century of Cricketers*, Harrap, 1950
Jim Parks (Editor), *The Book of Cricket*, Stanley Paul, 1962
The Nawab of Pataudi, *Tiger's Tale*, Stanley Paul, 1969
Barry Richards, *Barry Richards on Cricket: Attack to Win*, Pelham Books, 1973
C. Robertson-Glasgow, *Cricket Prints*, T. Werner Laurie, 1943 (Reprinted by permission of A. D. Peters and Co Ltd)
E. W. Swanton, *Cricket From All Angles*, Michael Joseph, 1968
E. W. Swanton and M. Melford, *The World of Cricket*, Michael Joseph, 1966
A. A. Thomson, *Hutton and Washbrook*, The Epworth Press, 1963

PHOTOGRAPHS

BBC Hulton Picture Library: pages 68, 69, 71 and 74
Central Press Photos: pages 6, 23, 24, 25, 34, 36, 40, 46, 48, 50 (left), 51, 65, 67, 72, 91, 98, 110, 111, 116 and 122
Colorsport: pages 21, 58, 89, 135 (right), 138, 141 and 148
Patrick Eagar: pages 28, 77, 79, 82, 86, 128, 135 (left), 137, 139 and 152
Adrian Murrell (Allsport Photographic): page 85
The Press Association: pages 27, 32, 38, 45, 53, 60, 76, 80, 94, 114, 118, 121, 124, 126, 127, 130, 145 and 155
Sport and General Press Agency: pages 20, 42, 43, 50 (right), 54, 99, 102, 103, 107, 108, 120, 133, 144, 151 and 156

JACKET

Action picture of Sir Donald Bradman by Sport and General, all others by Patrick Eagar.